# LIVING ARTFULLY
## At Home with Marjorie Merriweather Post

# LIVING ARTFULLY

### At Home with Marjorie Merriweather Post

Estella M. Chung

Hillwood Museum and Gardens Foundation, Washington, D.C.
in association with D Giles Limited, London

© 2013 Hillwood Museum and Gardens Foundation

First published in 2013 by GILES
An imprint of D Giles Limited
4 Crescent Stables, 139 Upper Richmond Road,
London, SW15 2TN, UK
www.gilesltd.com

Library of Congress Cataloging-in-Publication Data

Chung, Estella M.
 Living artfully : at home with Marjorie Merriweather Post / Estella M. Chung.
   pages cm
 Includes bibliographical references and index.
 ISBN 978-1-907804-13-7 (hardcover : alk. paper) — ISBN 978-1-931485-10-4
 (softcover : alk. paper)
 1. Post, Marjorie Merriweather. 2. Philanthropists—United States—Biography.
 3. Rich people—United States—Biography. 4. Hillwood Museum and Gardens—
 History. 5. Mar-A-Lago National Historic Site (Palm Beach, Fla.)—History. I.
 Hillwood Museum and Gardens. II. Title.
 HV28.P6C47 2013
 361.7'4092—dc23
 [B]
                    2012046251

ISBN (hardcover): 978-1-907804-13-7
ISBN (softcover): 978-1-931485-10-4

All rights reserved

No part of the contents of this book may be reproduced, stored in a retrieval system, or transmitted in any form or by any means, electronic, mechanical, photocopying, recording, or otherwise, without the written permission of the Trustees of Hillwood Museum and Gardens Foundation and D Giles Limited.

For Hillwood Museum and Gardens Foundation:
Kate Markert, Director, Hillwood Estate, Museum & Gardens
Liana Paredes, Director of Collections and Chief Curator
Estella M. Chung, Head of Oral History and Curator of American Material Culture and Historian
Photography by Ed Owen, John Dean, Alex Jamison and La Placa Cohen

For D Giles Limited:
Copyedited and proofread by Sarah Kane, Designed by Alfonso Iacurci
Produced by GILES, an imprint of D Giles Limited, London
Printed and bound in China

Front cover: Marjorie Post and Gus Modig reviewing the table before the start of a dinner party
Back cover: Round-and-square dance in Mar-A-Lago pavilion, 1964
Frontispiece: Setting Marjorie Post's table at Mar-A-Lago

# Contents

Foreword: Kate Markert, executive director     7

Acknowledgments     8

# Introduction     11

# Social Hillwood – Spring     23

# Camp Topridge – Summer     51

# Private Hillwood – Autumn     73

# Mar-A-Lago – Winter     99

Endnotes     129

Bibliography     135

Photo credits     141

Index     142

*opposite*
Post shows decorative arts collection
to high school students, 1963

# Foreword

In 1957, when Marjorie Merriweather Post established Hillwood as her primary residence and filled it with her magnificent collections of Russian Imperial art and spectacular French eighteenth- and nineteenth-century decorative art, she was seventy years old. She knew that the lifestyle she led was, in her words, "fast disappearing."

There had never been many people who lived quite as artfully as Marjorie Post. From decades of passionate collecting, she surrounded herself with superb works of art. Rather than storing her treasures away, she lived among them. As a private citizen, she entertained at a level and with a consistency comparable to that of heads of state. She moved from one fantastic estate to another as the seasons changed, from Hillwood in the spring to Camp Topridge in the summer, to Hillwood again in the autumn and then Mar-A-Lago for winter, each with its own collections and very special features.

From our very pragmatic twenty-first-century American viewpoint, we cannot help but wonder, "How did she do it?" Her skills in planning were legendary: she was able to conceptualize an entire project, be it a home, an over 300 foot sailing yacht, or a sparkling garden party down to the last perfect detail. She drew on her virtually unlimited resources, used very intentionally to produce the splendid effect she envisioned. We are the lucky inheritors of her meticulous planning and magnificent vision.

We are also fortunate that Marjorie Post left a wealth of documentation from her homes. Author Estella M. Chung, Head of Oral History and Curator of American Material Culture, has drawn on Hillwood's oral history collection, archives, and research sources in the American Midwest and East, as well as her own interviews with those who knew Post—from her daughter, actress Dina Merrill, to many of her staff and guests. By revealing the inner workings of her households, Estella Chung enables us to see what it took to produce this magnificent lifestyle.

We are very grateful to Harlan and Kathy Crow, the current owners of Camp Topridge, for their support of this publication.

**Kate Markert**
*Executive Director*
Hillwood Estate, Museum and Gardens
Washington, D.C.

# Acknowledgments

"As far as Marjorie Post's diary is concerned," I revealed to Hillwood's loyal group of volunteers, "I didn't locate one." I sighed as a hush washed across the auditorium, "I even checked behind the Beauvais tapestry in the French drawing room, inside the Monigetti cabinet in the Russian icon room, and the secret compartments of her Roentgen desk." And while the volunteers chuckled, their somewhat disappointed feelings matched mine at the conclusion that, so far, a deeply introspective journal by Post is yet to be found. Fortunately what remains is a multitude of personal memos and the reflections of people who spent time with Post—for her thoughtfulness and commanding presence were not easily forgotten.

*Living Artfully*, a topic-focused personal history of Post at her estates, could not have been published without the help of many people. Thank you to Harlan and Kathy Crow who granted generous access to present-day Camp Topridge and shared their wholehearted appreciation of the camp's history. Also at Topridge, much gratitude goes to Sue Jackman and Lawrence Lester for their hospitality and expertise. In Palm Beach, thank you to the Trump Organization for special entry to Mar-A-Lago hosted by Bernd Lembcke and Gloria Myers. To Francis Blouin, Karen Jania, and Malgosia Myc at the University of Michigan's Bentley Historical Library, thank you for the days and hours with the Post Family Collection.

In the District, appreciation goes to Nuchhi Currier and Jewell Fenzi for time in the Woman's National Democratic Club archives. Furthermore, thank you to Dina Merrill Hartley, as well as Harlan and Kathy Crow, for their thoughtful loans to the exhibition.

Many thanks to those who granted Hillwood oral history interviews, sharing their conversations with Post, observations of how she worked, and their impressions of her artful way of life. Their names are cited throughout *Living Artfully* and in the bibliography. Further gratitude goes to all of our oral history interviewees on various topics; their contributions are lasting records for the future. I speak for prior Hillwood oral historians Nancy Harris, Kathi Ann Brown, Stephanie Brown, and myself when I say that it was our honor to record your history with Marjorie Merriweather Post.

At Hillwood, my appreciation goes to board members, staff, and volunteers who shared enthusiasm and vision in this endeavor: Mrs. Ellen Charles, president of the board of trustees; Kate Markert, executive director; Angie Dodson, chief operations officer, director of interpretation and visitor services; Audra Kelly, head of interpretation and her staff; Judith Paska, director of development; and Lynn Rossotti, director of marketing and communications. My gratitude also goes to Hillwood alumni Fred Fisher, Joan Wetmore, and Michael Kruelle. A very special thanks to my enthusiastic colleagues and collaborators in the collections division, headed by Liana Paredes: Kirsten Regina, Ren Waung, Scott Ruby, Howard Kurtz, Pat Lynagh, Marla DiVietro, Manuel Rouco, Manuel Diaz, M. J. Meredith, Rebecca Petillo, and the late Anne Odom. Moreover, I am thankful to visitor services staff and volunteers extraordinaires, like Marilyn Uveges, for alerting me to people who revealed, "I knew Mrs. Post", and just so happened to be in Hillwood's gardens with friends and family, allowing us to identify additional oral history candidates.

Admiration and appreciation goes to photographers Edward Owen, John Dean, and Alex Jamison for capturing objects and spaces at Hillwood and Camp Topridge. The same also goes to publisher D Giles Limited in London, including Dan Giles, Sarah McLaughlin, Pat Barylski, editor Sarah Kane, and designer Alfonso Iacurci. I also thank my husband Matthew Brookman, extended family, and dear friends for their support while I happily worked away on this project.

To my colleagues in oral history, material culture, cultural history, and biography, I want to express my gratitude for eagerly sharing your knowledge and camaraderie. Cheers to members of the Biographers International Organization, headed by James McGrath Morris; and the Washington Biographers Group, guided by Marc Pachter and Pat McNees. Here's to the Material Culture Caucus of the American Studies Association and sharing inspiration with Deborah Andrews, Shirley Wajda, Sarah Carter, Bess Williamson, and Susan Garfinkel; I cannot forget the many fruitful conversations at the Oral History Association and Oral History in the Mid-Atlantic Region meetings. And I send much appreciation to the Smithsonian's National Museum of American History Colloquium, organized by David Haberstich and Roger Sherman, for sharing and vetting ideas.

Last but far from least, thank you to the board of trustees of the Hillwood Museum and Gardens Foundation, and Harlan and Kathy Crow for their generous funding and sponsoring of *Living Artfully*; it was a genuine pleasure to research and write about a woman for whom, as *Life* magazine correspondent David Zeitlin put it, "there is no letting down."

**Estella M. Chung**
*Head of Oral History*
*Curator of American Material*
*Culture and Historian*
Hillwood Estate,
Museum and Gardens
Washington, D.C.

# LIVING ARTFULLY

## Introduction

Porcelain storage cabinet

Post in General Foods' test kitchen

In 1969, shortly after her husband B. K. was sworn in as governor, Fori Nehru settled in the Raj Bhavan, the official residence of the Assam government, and wrote to Marjorie Merriweather Post, "Darling, darling Marjorie, when I said that I thought of you often, they were not empty words but a fact. So often your beautiful home, your orderly pantries, and silver cup-boards were before my eyes in comparison to what I have to contend with in my two government abodes."[1] By that time Post had been at the helm of several personal estates for six decades and was, at that moment, running three properties. From 1957 onwards she lived in the stately Hillwood in Washington, D.C. for spring and autumn, retreated to Camp Topridge in the Adirondacks for the summer, and enjoyed the winter season at her glamorous Mar-A-Lago in Palm Beach.

Marjorie Merriweather Post (1887–1973), an only child, inherited the Postum Cereal Company after her parents, Ella Merriweather and Charles William, passed in 1912 and 1914 respectively. Her father, who went by the moniker "C.W.," started the enterprise with Postum, a non-caffeinated coffee substitute, and the business grew with subsequent products such as Grape Nuts and Post Toasties. Continuing with key acquisitions in the 1920s, including Hellman's Mayonnaise, Sanka, Jell-O, Log Cabin Syrup, Maxwell House Coffee, and the risky-yet-innovative concept of frosted foods by Clarence Birdseye, the company became General Foods in 1929.[2] Still involved with the corporation as director emerita, Post weighed in on product development and even returned an unsatisfactory box of Sugar Crisp cereal to General Foods' research manager in 1962.[3]

In 1966, the *Boston Globe* called Post the most quoted woman millionaire, as she was prominent not only for her role within

Post's "Hillwood service" by Gorham

Post's room in The Boulders

*My room in "The Boulders"*

General Foods, but also for philanthropic fundraising, which often included opening her homes in support of American and international causes.[4] Newspaper clippings recounting her charitable and social functions fill scrapbook upon scrapbook, describing her as a fabulous hostess and noting the remarkable administration of her homes. As the *New York Times* put it, "Mrs. Post's life is as orderly as it is luxurious."[5]

Her artful way of living came with practice. "The operation of my household is the result of careful planning over the many years," she wrote in 1965, "each house is an entity, with its own equipment for that particular spot and environment."[6] Sixty years earlier, her very first estate, The Boulders in Greenwich, Connecticut had a house staff of fourteen and nearly sixty workers beautifying the grounds. Post remembered her father saying, "These workers have to be paid every week and I want an account and it's got to be balanced at the end of the summer."[7] He also gave her an allowance with budget allocations for investing, household expenses, and personal expenses. When she was four cents short in her accounting book, C.W. was not satisfied, "I worked like a dog and of course found it finally and so that was acceptable," said Post, "I lost twenty-seven pounds that year."[8]

In 1964 *Life* magazine correspondent David Zeitlin asked her, "Do you ever get the feeling that having a large staff is really more trouble than it's worth?" At age seventy-seven Post replied, "It's no trouble to me, you see I have done this kind of thing since I was 18 and it rolls right off my back."[9] While also amassing a collection of French and Russian decorative arts, Post easily managed a private Pullman train car, a triplex apartment in Manhattan with fifty-four rooms, a 176 acre country estate on Long Island, two ambassador's residences, an Adirondack camp, a Palm Beach mansion, and an astonishingly well-appointed four-masted sailing ship, among other residences before she came to an established rotation between her Washington, D.C., Adirondack, and Palm Beach homes.[10]

Catherine the Great Easter egg, Fabergé 1914

*opposite*
Dining table set with Sèvres porcelain at Hillwood

*left*     Post with daughters Adelaide, Nedenia, and Eleanor
*below*    Chair covers used when Post not in residence

With first husband, attorney Edward Close, she had daughters Adelaide and Eleanor Close. With second spouse, financier E. F. Hutton, her third and youngest child, Nedenia Hutton, later to become the actress Dina Merrill. Upon her divorce to American ambassador to the Soviet Union and Belgium, Joseph Davies, she purchased Hillwood in Washington, D.C., which she then shared with her fourth husband, businessman Herbert May. With the exception of her six-year marriage to Herbert May, the other unions spanned fourteen to twenty years. She always took a new married name, but ultimately returned to Marjorie Post after her last divorce in 1964.[11] Post told a friend, "You know I've been very smart about most everything in my life, but I'm not smart about men."[12] Her granddaughter Ellen Charles reflected, "I guess you can't have everything, and she certainly did enjoy herself most of the time."[13]

Post excelled at working with her staff to run her estates, social, business, and philanthropic life. Whether married, or back to being Mrs. Post, "it was her home, definitely," clarified Mar-A-Lago superintendent Jimmy Griffin.[14] By 1957 her annual routine of moving from Washington, D.C. to the Adirondacks, back to the District of Columbia, and then to Palm Beach ran with precision. Up to four chauffeurs, two secretaries, two personal maids, and a masseur traveled with her to each home, while a skeleton crew went on ahead to open each property in advance and another stayed behind to take care of closing the other home, in which the location of everything was noted and put away.[15] "Every chair had its own little chintz cover that went over it and had a number, every picture had a number on the back, and what table it went to because

*opposite*
Before closing a home, all objects including picture frames were noted

*left*
*Merriweather* jet takes guests to Camp Topridge

*middle*
Interior *Merriweather* turboprop jet, 1969

*right*
Interior, *Merriweather* turboprop jet

we didn't have Polaroids in those days," laughed daughter Dina Merrill Hartley, "oh, it was something."[16] Superintendent Jimmy Griffin added, "Everything [was returned to] exactly the way she left it, and believe me she knew."[17]

In between seasons Post traveled, or went to a resort in Virginia or Arkansas.[18] Supervisors working for Post estimated she employed between 100 to 300 people across her residences in full-time, part-time, or seasonal positions—it varied depending on the year's activities.[19] "She didn't mind living in a fishbowl [and] when you have as much staff as she had, you're never really alone," reflected house party guest Spottswood Dudley, "she did not run a house, she ran a hotel."[20] A general manager and financial office worked closely with Post to oversee the account ledgers of all properties.

Her staff came from international placement agencies or locally, creating a workplace with American, Scottish, Irish, Italian, Norwegian, Polish, German, and Cuban employees.[21]

Connecting each residence was a fleet of thirty-four vehicles and the *Merriweather* turboprop jet, a reconfigured forty-four capacity plane with carefully selected fabrics from Scalamandré made spacious for seventeen passengers.[22] Gabriele Weinert, a personal maid who traveled with Post to each property, explained, "My clothes and everything was taken care of by the chauffeurs

*top*     Square-dance outfits packed in Louis Vuitton trunk
*bottom*   Trunks indicating Hillwood mansion rooms

and most of the staff was going by the *Merriweather* airplane, it really was fun."²³ The chauffeurs drove Plymouth, Pontiac, Dodge, Oldsmobile, Cadillac, and Chrysler station wagons, luxury sedans, and limousines to the next home. After taking a flight back, they then repeated delivering vehicles until they had what they needed. Post preferred a customized 1964 Cadillac series 75 limousine and Cadillac Fleetwood Brougham car. To accommodate her hats, the limousine roof was raised five inches over her passenger seat. When someone asked one of her drivers, Frank Del Monte, "How come Mrs. Post doesn't have a Rolls Royce?" he replied, "With a Cadillac I can go to a Chevrolet dealer and they can repair me . . . if we had a Rolls Royce and I broke down somewhere in New England, I'd have to wait until [they] took it all the way to Washington."²⁴ Between the modes of ground transportation and the private plane, orchids, congressmen, generals, fashion house designers with dress samples, a live model to show dress samples, ambassadors, and grandchildren were transported smoothly between the seasons and long-weekend getaways to stay with Post.²⁵

    Being forthright, many of Marjorie Post's staff and guests granted oral history interviews to Hillwood historians with the intention of thanking her, summing up her qualities as "able to talk to anyone at any

Tall-hatted Post at British embassy

"Post stood up for her people extremely well . . . she recognized that the way to run a household was that you had to appease everyone."

level, cheerful, and a great lady."[26] She was a competitive employer, offering up to thirty-five percent higher compensation and generous perks paid on the estate account; she also took charge of critical-care medical expenses for staff, while providing group health insurance in later years.[27] Interviewees also paraphrased their conversations with Post, giving glimpses into her sense of humor, idiosyncrasies, kindnesses, and interests.

Overall, Post successfully balanced personalities with requirements and structure. As head of the estate, in addition to seeing to the paperwork, financial manager Donald Handelman felt Post "stood up for her people extremely well . . . she recognized that the way to run a household was that you had to

Drawing of modified limousine roof

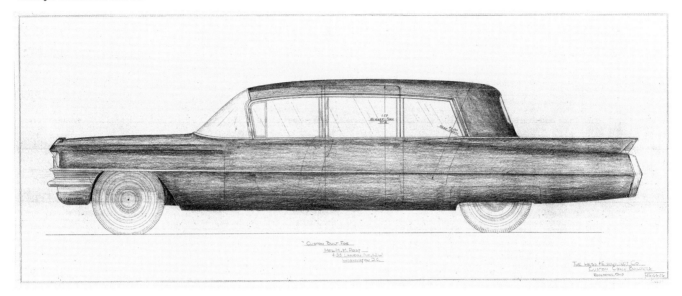

appease everyone."²⁸ In turn, each staff member had his or her main duties, and Post had no problem delegating and instilling a sense that she expected assignments to be carried out, whatever they may be. "Another interesting thing," continued Donald, was that she used "whatever channel of command she had established . . . she didn't jump around and try to skip or go over somebody's head . . . she kept to that routine—there are not many people I have met in my lifetime that could."²⁹ Stepgranddaughter Jennifer Conover evaluated, "You know, it's funny, she was, I think, difficult in one sense, but in another sense terribly easy, because she seemed to be able to inspire the same kind of perfectionism from others that she fully expected of herself."³⁰ Jennifer continued, "She saw to people's needs in a lovely kind of way, and, of course, that instilled great love for her from a lot of people."³¹

The elaborate nature of her lifestyle did not preclude practicality, from her insistence on planning and organization to her commonsense approach to looking after her properties; as she explained in 1964, "If you keep things up it's much less expensive than if you let it go and then you've got to do the whole thing over . . . it really pays in the long run."³² Post's method of maintaining a financial and material legacy ultimately resulted in her leaving Hillwood to the public as a museum. She wanted people to enjoy her decorative arts collection and be able to take a closer look at her lifestyle. In her later years she often said to her financial manager, "I want young Americans to see how someone lived in the twentieth century and how this person could collect works of art the way I have . . . I want to share this with the rest of the world. Maybe it'll be an incentive to some people. Maybe it won't, but at least they'll get a chance to see how I lived."³³

# SOCIAL HILLWOOD

## Spring

*opposite*
Butler Gus Modig

top    Aerial view of Hillwood showing the motor court
bottom    Peruvian ambassador (right) among guests at Hillwood, 1957

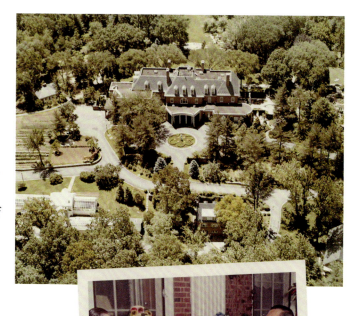

With her staff, Marjorie Merriweather Post organized delightful spring garden teas for literally hundreds of Washingtonian guests. Yet it did not end with teas: invitations to formal dinners at Hillwood were also highly prized. "Mrs. Post" was one of the top Washington hostesses, during an era when this was an especially high aspiration for women. She and her staff were in the public eye with parties, dinners, and charitable events from the time Post opened Hillwood in 1957 until her death in 1973. "Now she never had servants. She had 'staff.' She never referred to them as servants," reminisced Post's grandson-in-law Rodion Cantacuzene, "They did everything they could to please her. Not through fear, but through honest affection."[1] Gus Modig was the majordomo of Hillwood in Washington, D.C. "He was devoted to her and she was to him," clarified Rodion.[2]

Gus Modig left Sweden in 1937, worked as a butcher, a valet, joined the American army and was discharged with citizenship papers in hand by 1947. In winter 1948, through a placement agency, he was offered a job at Post's Palm Beach estate as a footman. "I did silver (polishing) and after that I became the guests' valet, pressing their clothes," explained Gus.[3] When Marjorie Post literally told Gus Modig in 1959, "You're going to take this job [the Hillwood butler position]," she asked what he would like to be called by the staff. He replied "Gus," and she suggested to the staff that they call him "Mr. Gus."[4]

Most often, Post's guests to Hillwood would be invited to a formal meal (lunch or dinner) or a garden tea. With Mr. Gus and social secretary Margaret Voigt, Post did much of her party planning from her dressing room. Mr. Gus remembered that, generally, the head of the house reeled off who was to be invited, rather than Margaret making suggestions. Additionally, Margaret kept track of Hillwood's menus, so as not to overly duplicate menu items with returning

```
E & G RUSSIAN PLATES
EAST 92nd ST PLATES
NICHOLAS 1st PLATES
MORGAN SEVRES BLUE
WEDDING GLASS
RUSSIAN GLOLD LACE TABLE CLOTHS
FRENCH SILVER SERVICE

RED ROSES
WHITE POM POMS
WHITE FUJIIS
WHIRE SMALL MUMS
```

**MENU**

*Caviar and Blinis*

*Roast Butter Ball Turkey*
*Chestnut Dressing      Lingonberry Sauce*
*Sweet Potatoes Marshmallow*
*Vegetable Jardiniere*

*Mixed Green Garden Salad*
*Brie*

*Apple Jello Ring with Assorted Fruit*
*Filled with Balls of Strawberry*
*Sherbert*

*Cup Cake          Cookies*

Vodka
Chassagne Montrachet 1953
Moet Chandon Dom Perignon 1952

HILLWOOD
October 17, 1963

*right*
List of dining services by meal course and flowers for the table

*bottom right*
Menu, 1963

Post's dressing room, 1970s

Garden tea, 1969

guests. Especially important for a dinner in Washington, a seating plan according to diplomatic protocols and escort cards was worked out.[5]

Post selected the linens, silver, and of course the porcelain for each dinner course. While a linen book was kept in the butler's pantry, indicating an identification number for each lace style, she knew them well enough to recall them from memory, but Mr. Gus used the linen book to confirm.[6] A serious collector of decorative art with a focus on French and Russian pieces, a dinner party guest at her table could enjoy not only the food, but also the visual experience created with eighteenth-century French dinner

# "Marjorie was a perfectionist from the word go."

services, German sterling silver hammered fruit compotes, a Russian Imperial military service that included forty-four plates, and lace runner mats, among many other splendid articles from her collection. In addition to being displayed throughout much of the mansion, a substantial portion of porcelain was kept in the basement porcelain storage cabinets and conveniently transported into the butler's pantry via a dumbwaiter. Footman Arthur Field, whose duties were to polish the silver, had easy access since the silver safe was also located in the pantry.[7]

Yet, not only was the exquisite artistry of the individual pieces unforgettable; their precision placement was newsworthy too. The *New York Times* in 1966 and *Life* magazine in 1965 printed details of how Mr. Gus and staff set the table.[8] On the morning of a formal dinner, they started marking off 8, 16, 18, or 20 inch spaces using measuring tapes or rulers and placing cards noting the perfectly symmetrical and equidistant locations for the plates, linens, and so forth. Mr. Gus said, "It took all of us there—it took a few hours—yes, it did."[9] Post reviewed the table twice, first earlier in the day, and then when she was dressed—sometimes tweaking a knife and fork, or a flower, but not making substantial adjustments. *Miami Herald* social columnist Suzy reported, "The overhang of

Linen book

Marjorie Post and Gus Modig reviewing the table before the start of a dinner party

*opposite*
Footman Arthur Field

*opposite*
Cooking for Post, staff, and guests

*top*
Family wedding luncheon honoring Cliff Robertson and daughter Dina Merrill, 1966

*middle*
Battle Creek High School students at Hillwood, 1963

*bottom*
Dining tables in contrasting color palettes

[Marjorie Post's] tablecloth was just as it should be, exactly the same on all sides."[10]

According to Mr. Gus, although it was not her typical style, the breadth of Post's glass and porcelain collection allowed for multiple tables featuring different color palettes in the dining room or Hillwood's pavilion.[11] The visual experience of the linens and porcelain formed indelible memories in the minds of her guests. Even decades later, after Post's passing in 1973, social columnist Betty Beale remembered:

> Marjorie was a perfectionist from the word go. No one has ever been . . . that organized, and that interested, all the way to the infinite detail . . . the way she loved to have one table so all the crystal was the lavender and the china would blend in of course. And then she'd have another table with red roses in the middle, and all of it would be the ruby crystal. And then she'd have one with yellow, yellow roses, or some yellow flower in the center.[12]

Others felt as guest and Hillwood neighbor Peggy Brown did, that "it was a shame to soil the beautiful linens."[13] Peggy added that it was a shock when another guest "took the plate and turned it over to see the mark on it."[14]

Ridgewells catering company provided extra dinner waiters. Each side of the table had a waiter for meat, another for vegetables and bread, as well as one for wine.[15] As social

# "I mean it was amazing, these were the French cut string beans. Just perfect soldiers lined up."

columnist Suzy described a meal at Hillwood, "There was a footman behind each person, as always, and individual menus for each person to peruse. So much chic-er than having just one at each table and having to pass it around, don't you find?"[16]

The extra waiters from Ridgewells did not clear the table of the dirty dishes that also happened to be Post's decorative arts collection, having been instructed not to touch anything on the table. That work was done by her own staff. For a large dinner, two housemen washed the dishes and two parlor maids dried them, the services then being put away immediately. "With the silver, you put it down, slowly, not dump it, you put it down, and there was a mat in the bottom of the sink . . . one by one, not a handful," clarified Mr. Gus, adding with a sense of humor, "We had to be careful. I still have the whip."[17] Things seldom got broken.

In addition to not clearing dishes, Mr. Gus recounted that Ridgewells did not do the cooking. Cooking was done at Hillwood.[18] The menu was seasonally influenced, for example new lamb or veal, and a particular holiday might call for suckling pig. Ellen Charles, Post's granddaughter, described the food and its presentation:

> Grandmother liked the finest quality food and simply prepared. So the food was wonderful . . . a beautifully cooked roast beef, or a wonderful tenderloin. And the string beans would come out and they were all perfectly lined up. I mean it was amazing, these were the French cut string beans. Just perfect soldiers lined up. The presentation was fabulous . . . there was never anything informal here if you came for a meal . . . it was always full service and beautiful porcelain . . . certainly all the men were in coat and ties . . . that's just the way things were here.[19]

In nationally syndicated newspapers, Post received attention as a supreme hostess. Seven East Coast newspapers printed, "If Mrs. Post says 'Formal' it IS Formal . . . You'd better believe it." Meaning that she and her dinner guests would dress appropriately, in long gowns.[20]

At Hillwood, cocktails were at 8 p.m., with guests entering through the bright and sparkling entry hall. After male guests had left their coats with a footman and female guests with the lady stationed in the powder room, staff announced guests to Post as they arrived. She greeted everyone in the French drawing room. The cocktail waiter took drink orders and prepared alcoholic beverages in the butler's pantry, using standard 1950s, '60s, and '70s cocktail glasses. According to Mr. Gus, Post had a cocktail glass with a little bit of Seagram's V.O. and water, "You probably could say the water is colored a little bit, and then she just took a little bit."[21] Although she

French drawing room, 1960s

Marjorie Merriweather Post at Hillwood, ca. 1957

practiced Christian Science, Post did drink small amounts of caffeine and alcohol.

At 8:30 p.m., the butler rang the dinner bell and each gentleman escorted his designated lady to her seat, as indicated on the seating chart. After the meal, guests separated for coffee, cigarettes, and more conversation. One guest, Walter Beach, recalled, "You know, she loved to talk about the products of her company . . . after dinner, of course they would serve decaffeinated coffee, Maxwell House, and Postum, and the butlers would ask which one would you have."[22] In the evening Marjorie Post drank Postum. Guests smoked at the dining table; each place setting included two cigarettes of different brands, with guests trading according to their preferences. For coffee, gentlemen remained in the dining room, and ladies went into the drawing room.

Often first-run films followed dinner, as the Hillwood pavilion movie equipment included anamorphic lenses for cinemascope projection. Staff watched from the balcony complete with movie theater seats.[23] In 1970, Post hosted a dinner at which the guests included a general, a baron, and the ambassador of the Soviet Union. The evening ended with a screening of Walt Disney's *The Jungle Book*.[24] Social columnist Betty Beale was critical of this aspect of receptions at Hillwood, "Washington is a very conversational town because of politics, and everybody wanted to get the latest inside scoop."[25] At Post's dinners, people could talk with guests seated next to them, but not with everyone at the gathering. "And Marjorie, after every dinner had a film," continued Beale, "you couldn't talk, and that was her one failing as a hostess."[26]

After the movie, staff served snacks to guests in the hallway outside the pavilion. Typically the evening was over by 11 p.m., which employees considered a perk of working at Hillwood, a reasonable time to end the work day considering that other households required hours past 2 a.m. Mr. Gus remembered that the evening concluded with a visit to the kitchen, "[Mrs. Post] went to the cook and thanked her very much, and sometimes they had a guest of honor and took them into the kitchen to say something."[27]

When in residence at Hillwood, usually in the spring and autumn, Post held dinners about once a month, three 125-person luncheons (mixing gentlemen and ladies, not exclusively a ladies' affair), and garden teas over a weekend.[28] The teas followed formal

Escort and menu card

Place setting including two cigarettes and matches

Pavilion with theater seating in balcony

Social Hillwood – Spring

Post with guest Louise McNutt, 1957

Pavilion, 1957

*left*
Icon room, 1970s

*below left*
Pull-out drawers with information about the objects above

*below*
Detail, estate sound system speaker locations

etiquette, with cards indicating who was to pour tea and who was to pour coffee and at which hours.[29] The parties included opportunities to peruse her impressive art collection, and guests made use of pull-out drawers in Post's display cabinets that contained information about the art objects.[30] Furthermore, stationed guides—friends or young people—answered questions about the collection. Meanwhile, the estate sound system piped music into the garden, dining room, library, drawing room, and pavilion.

For Post, hosting parties was entirely voluntary, and the pleasure they gave her more than compensated for the expense and hard work involved. Social columnist Betty Beale observed, "[Marjorie] wore a look of amused delight when watching the fun her guests were having. She derived real fulfillment from using her money that way."[31] According to Perle Mesta (the Hostess with the Mostess), "In an atmosphere of good food, music, and gracious women, differences sometimes can be settled or important matters of policy worked out . . . [but] much of the benefit may be indirect . . . friendships made at parties turn out to be helpful years later."[32] Turning many individual decisions such as guest lists, table settings, menus, color schemes, and flowers into a cohesive, comfortable, interesting, convivial and enjoyable event was a great deal of work, but the goal was to make it seamless. "Social life . . . is part of the art of living in Washington," remarked Jackie Kennedy.[33]

However, the usefulness of parties in the nation's capital was not clear to everyone; when descriptions of such parties were syndicated in large- and small-town newspapers across

Motor court leading to front door of the mansion

# "The soda was for servicemen invited to Hillwood in the late 1960s and into the early 1970s for cocktails, luncheon, musical entertainment, and to enjoy the gardens and Post's art collection."

the country, without any explanation of the short- or long-term benefit of Washington social life, columnists received letters of complaint from readers across the nation about frivolous Washingtonian party-going. Betty Beale challenged these complaints, wondering what good could result if officials went "straight home and moped all evening about the world situation. If someone asked you to a party would you decline because the world is in a bad situation? And if you did, would it help the world any?"[34]

Post was in her seventies in the 1960s and for women of her generation, being a renowned hostess and being married to someone prominent was a high distinction. "We were very much part of our husband's life . . . it never occurred to us to be looked down upon," reflected diplomatic corps spouse Elizabeth Moffat White.[35] But there were hostesses contemporary with Post who belonged to another generation. To illustrate the difference, Jackie Kennedy and many Georgetown-based party-givers were in their thirties and forties. For some of the younger generation, the term "hostess" and the role of being the wife of a high-profile man was still held in high regard, but under review in terms of autonomy and professionalization. Wives were becoming tired of being asked, "So what does your husband think?" Evangeline Bruce, wife of a United States envoy, referred to "hostess" as "the H word." She clarified, "Hostess—that one I really resent

. . . [I was expected] to be solely responsible for all diplomatic entertaining . . . what I do is run the social wing of the embassy."[36] Outside Washington, the transitioning roles of women received acknowledgement as well. By the late 1950s, mass-market cookbooks included tips for "how to market when you have a job" and commented that, "The cook is also housemaid, chambermaid, waitress, nurse, chauffeur, gardener—as well as wife, mother, job-holder, and community leader."[37]

During Post's years of running Hillwood, there were four first ladies in the White House, and undoubtedly the first lady was the leading hostess of the District. Marjorie Post had cordial relations with Mamie Eisenhower, Jackie Kennedy, Lady Bird Johnson, and Pat Nixon. She received an official invitation to Eisenhower's inauguration ceremony, with Mamie's "hope that you will be the personal guest of Ike and myself."[38] The "President and Mrs. Kennedy requested the pleasure of [her] company" on April 30, 1963 at 8 p.m.[39] Post enjoyed watercress soup and chicken crepes at a White House luncheon with Lady Bird Johnson, presumably for the "More Beautiful Capital" project.[40] Being a regular White House guest and a hostess herself, she could not help but add to a thank-you note to Mrs. Nixon, "[I] was so pleased to see the dinner tables arranged again as they have not been in such a while."[41] Even with White House invitations, Post had

Veteran and Vietnam-wounded guests at Hillwood

sufficient stature and rapport to be able to decline offers with regret when she had prior engagements. Like all invitations to Post, they were coordinated with social secretary Margaret Voigt, who reviewed requests with the lady of the house and responded on her behalf.[42]

In addition to the causes grandly and officially promoted at the White House, Post and staff vetted requests from other Washington, D.C. organizations.[43] The Woman's National Democratic Club not only received new furnishings for their main drawing room in 1966, but also a silver tray with matching bowl and a plethora of fine linens. The *Washington Post* reported that, in addition to a gift, Mrs. Post also gave a laundry lesson.[44] As she presented the gift, Marjorie Post shared her linen care tips with the ladies at the club. "There is one way to remove wine spots … [and] another way to get out grease or vegetable stains," Post told them, revealing, "I have cloths which have never been laundered after 40 years of use."[45] The head gardener at Hillwood, Earl Loy, remembered that, if anything was on her tablecloths, "she would take a little saucer [or have the butler do it] and put cold water . . . and that would take the stain out. But she'd do it that very night."[46]

"It was heartwarming to see—those Coke bottles on the dining room table," recalled Hillwood neighbor Peggy Brown.[47] The soda was for servicemen invited to Hillwood in the late 1960s and into the early 1970s for cocktails, luncheon, musical entertainment, and to enjoy the gardens and Post's art collection. Although the day and month changed over time, that year she and her staff organized three May garden parties on Saturday, Sunday, and eventually designated Monday for the military—taking advantage of the spring weather and already having tents assembled and silver polished.[48] While one *Washington Post* writer celebrated the elegance of Saturday and Sunday garden teas, describing the events as refreshing "in this day of be-ins, sit-ins, wade-ins, protests, marches, and happenings," Post's grandson-in-law Rodion Cantacuzene explained that the special invitations to wounded Vietnam veterans at Walter Reed Army Hospital and Bethesda Naval Hospital meant a great deal in the context of returning home to the United States:[49]

[She] was a patriotic American woman . . . I mean, if everyone had felt that way, the servicemen would have felt a lot better about the Vietnamese War and they wouldn't have felt so insulted. These young gentlemen came back, [and] no one was there to cheer them . . . And they were spat upon and they were shouted at and they were called murderers and killers and things like that. She didn't.⁵⁰

Underlining the desire for warm receptions at home was the Marine Corps request to photograph and print a story about the Hillwood tea in their *Leatherneck* magazine, distributed to American soldiers in Vietnam. The photography request stated, "It would mean very much to them to read about the attention that is given those who have served their country in battle."⁵¹ By July 1969, over half the patients at Walter Reed Army Hospital had served in Vietnam. When the wounded arrived at Hillwood in wheelchairs and on crutches, Mr. Gus told Post, "There are some stretchers and things out there." She replied, "Don't worry about that, that's okay."⁵²

Another local and national cause Post believed in—an expression of cultural patriotism— was her "Music for Young America" series with the National Symphony. Howard Mitchell, music director of the symphony, felt young people visiting the capital should hear their national orchestra. As patron, Post hoped it would prompt young people to seek good music, support local orchestras, or start one. A sampling of the 1959 program included Brahms's *Andante sostenuto from Symphony No. 1*, Mozart's *Minuetto from Divertimento No. 17*, and Ravel's *Finale "General Dance" from Daphnis and Chloe, Suite No. 2*.⁵³ Newspaper reporter Donnie Radcliffe called Post

the "Belle of Umpteen Symphony Balls" for her support of the NSO that not only included the series, but also gala tables, and an eighteen-carat gold Cartier bracelet with ninety-six diamonds for the fundraising auction.⁵⁴

As a tribute, the symphony played "Happy Birthday" to Marjorie Merriweather Post for her eightieth birthday in March 1967, a special moment that had been coordinated between symphony staff and social secretary Margaret Voigt. Vice president and Mrs. Humphrey as well as others gave their boxes for the occasion, while the Women's Committee for the symphony decorated the boxes for Post and guests with flowers. They also played a special request—Hindemith's *Hérodiade*— conducted by her son-in-law Leon Barzin. Post's ticket from that evening at Constitution Hall remains in her scrapbook.⁵⁵ Later that year, in July 1967, the new amphitheater in Columbia, Maryland, to be the summer home of the orchestra, was named the Merriweather Post Pavilion of Music after

*left*     Symphony boxes specially decorated for Post's eightieth birthday, 1967
*below*    Post hosts Battle Creek High School students, 1963

"one of Washington's most generous music enthusiasts."⁵⁶ When an inspired visitor to the pavilion wrote to Post about the pavilion being "possible through your generous gift," Post wrote back, "I should correct the impression you seem to have about the auditorium . . . [the symphony] paid me the very great honor . . . I am deeply touched that it bears my name."⁵⁷ Despite hopes that she would, Marjorie Merriweather Post did not specifically fund the pavilion.⁵⁸

Post's relationship with the Kennedy family was social, and with Rose Kennedy in particular, supportive. Of the same generation, and roughly three years apart in age, they exchanged telegrams and letters sharing the joys and tragedies that Rose experienced with her politician sons. Rose wrote, "[I received] your cable sent at the time of Jack's nomination. Thank you very much, dear Marjorie, for thinking of us at that time. It was wonderful to know that our friends were rejoicing with us."⁵⁹ In March 1968 Rose wrote to Post, "The campaign seems much more of a responsibility than the one in 1960. However, I know that Bobby is very sincere about his goals and will work very hard, and so we are always optimistic."⁶⁰ And sadly, upon Bobby's assassination just a few months later, in June 1968, Post's telegram to Rose read, "My heart aches for you with this added tragedy."⁶¹ Rose replied, "I know it came straight from your heart and my heart responded with affection and appreciation."⁶²

Some visitors to Hillwood had nothing to do with Washington politics or society, but were special educational and philanthropic guests who could expect to enjoy a jaw-dropping experience. When Post met the sorority sisters of Sigma Alpha Theta at C. W. Post College of Long University she said, "Oh, what a lovely group of young ladies. You must come to Washington."⁶³ What was even more astonishing was the opportunity to be photographed for *Life* magazine at Hillwood. "She agreed to have *Life* magazine come

Post shows art collection to high school students, 1963

Student guests in the French parterre, 1963

… she thought it would help promote the college and she was all for that," explained sorority member Lisa Smith.[64] In the article titled, "Sorority Sisters' Luxury Weekend," *Life* printed, "Awed by it all, the girls at first talked only in whispers."[65] Lisa recalled, "I guess that's true [that the sisters spoke in whispers] … we were just so impressed with everything."[66] Post flew the young ladies to Washington by private plane, put them up at a hotel, provided local transportation by private bus, served them a formal lunch in the Hillwood dining room, gave tours of her decorative arts collection and gardens, and hosted a mock-cocktail party in Hillwood's pavilion.

"We were not, you know, society girls," explained Lisa, "for some of us we might have been the first woman or first person in our families to go to college."[67] Some of the sisters had suits and hats for church that were appropriate, but Lisa Smith remembered shopping especially for the trip to Washington, "Being Jewish I didn't go to church and I didn't have hats."[68] Marjorie Post also dressed for the occasion and wore suits and an evening gown.

*Life* printed the article in the May 16, 1960 issue. There was not a picture in the magazine spread of Post alone. "Every picture has all of us … she was very clear on that … and occasionally I would hear her, if they wanted to take a picture [of just Mrs. Post] … and she would make us come closer," explained Lisa.[69] The tradition of a grand tour of Washington for the sisters carried on, and special invitations were also extended to C.W. Post College Sigma Alpha Epsilon fraternity and Battle Creek High School students. Yet, Post wanted the trips to be a treat and a reward. She instructed Ginger Barbara, president of the sorority in 1968, "The way to pick [the twenty-four sisters for the trip] is the highest academic standing and no dues unpaid."[70]

Like the 1960 *Life* article, Marjorie Post approached the 1965 piece showcasing her philanthropic spirit and estates with equal discretion and savvy towards print media. Namely, she made it clear to *Life* correspondent David Zeitlin that she wanted to review the text to check for errors and that she did not want the story to be "blatty" or "dangling of dollar signs."[71] *Life* assigned photographer Alfred Eisenstaedt, known for his 1945 image of a celebratory sailor kissing a nurse in Times Square. After the article ran in the November 5, 1965 issue, Zeitlin acknowledged that working with Post was rewarding, recognizing her kindness, consideration, "and also your great sense of discipline … in an era like ours, it was inspiring to meet a lady in whom there is no letting down."[72]

*Life* was very successful in conveying warmth and even too much approachability.[73] Enough letters were sent to Post in response to the article that staff had to organize them alphabetically by state or by foreign country. Much of the mail arrived without the official address for any of her homes, but rather a description based on the article. Airmail addressed to "Mrs. Marjorie Merriweather Post, Palm Beach, Rockcreek

Post gives Lady Bird Johnson a garden tour, 1966

## "Each and every one of us, regardless, have our trials and tribulations and in my lifetime I have had very many..."

Park, U.S.A" and "Georgian Mansion, Hillwood, Washington, D.C." reached Post and staff from India, Gambia, and Malawi.[74]

Letters requesting financial assistance, or even asking point blank, "Would you consider giving me a million dollars?" were kindly acknowledged by general manager Clyde Ault, who indicated with regret that Post's charitable and educational commitments were ones she had supported for many years and new gifts were not possible no matter how deserving.[75] From Bangalore, a mill worker wrote, "I am the head of a family of six persons [with one boy in college] … I want to increase my earning by undertaking extra part-time jobs … for example I can take up typing jobs."[76] He asked for an old or second-hand typewriter. She sent a Smith Corona portable typewriter to him.

A woman in Texas wrote, "Your fortune must be a wonderful feeling to know you don't have any worries—I have never been that lucky."[77] The woman continued to outline her plans to retire and hopes to own a new car some day. Post firmly replied:

> What you had to say about "worries" interested me greatly. Believe me, just because I happen to be me and you are you, does not for one minute mean that I do not have my worries, too. Each and every one of us, regardless, have our trials and tribulations and in my lifetime I have had very many and sometimes they have been difficult to overcome. Position is relative, and each one of us must carry our own peculiar burden . . . living takes courage and fortitude for all of us, and I am sure you have this in full measure."[78]

With Hillwood dinners and garden teas in the newspapers, and Post pictured with staff in the internationally distributed *Life* magazine, it was understood that Hillwood was a place in the public eye—appreciated for its perfection in all things, down to the spacing between salad and dinner forks. The staff knew this. "Hillwood is one of the Nation's showplaces … consequently the estate is constantly subject to unexpected inspection and scrutiny not only by the owner but by outsiders," wrote general manager James Mann to the staff, "your cooperation in maintaining the service building in the Hillwood tradition will be appreciated."[79] Lady Bird Johnson noted admiringly that everything Marjorie Post "touches seems to turn to beauty."[80] And without fail, thanks to tight organization, down to the last wash basin in the service building, Hillwood was indeed a beautiful place.

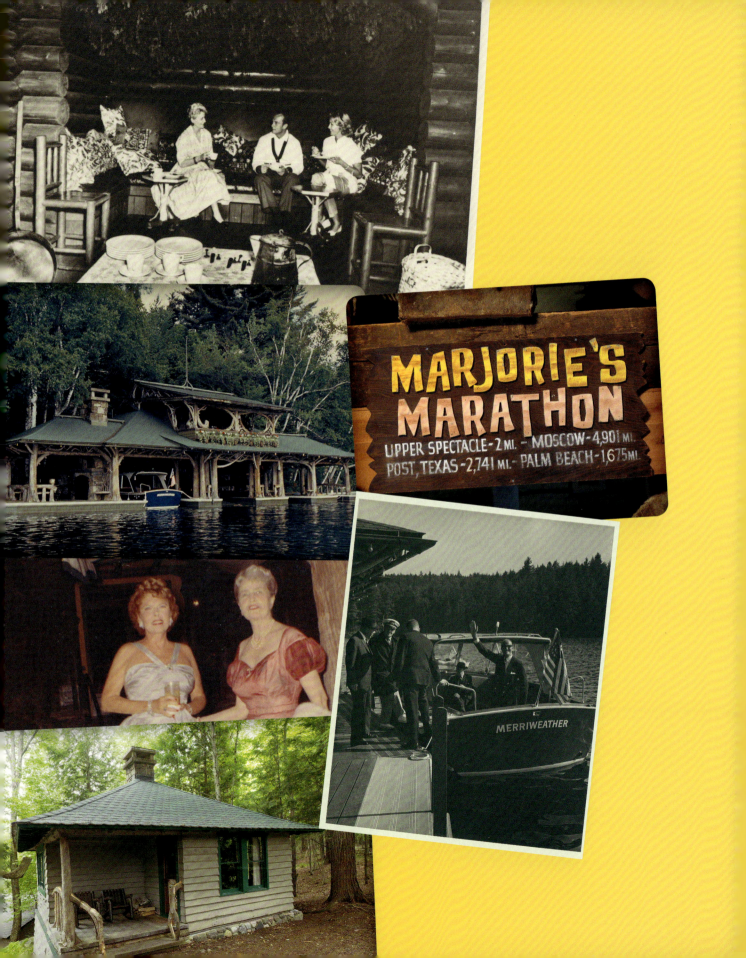

# CAMP TOPRIDGE

## Summer

View of Spectacle Lake from Camp Topridge's main lodge

"I loved Camp, loved it!" reminisced actress Dina Merrill, the youngest of Marjorie Post's three daughters, "canoeing, frog-hunting, going on picnics with my mother—she made her famous Adirondack pie—it was positively delicious!"[1] With Post operating Topridge since 1920, several generations, including grandchildren Ellen Charles, Nina Rumbough, and Stanley Rumbough enthusiastically enjoyed Camp. "Especially when I was younger, the Adirondacks was my most favorite of all grandmother's homes, it was a wonderful place for kids," reflected Ellen.[2] "We had fabulous times at Camp," expressed Nina, "the fishing, swimming, the slide into the lake—the whole feel of the place was fun."[3] Camp Topridge was "this huge wonderful place with all kinds of possibilities for hide-and-go-seek," described Stanley.[4]

Washington officials were equally enthusiastic about retreating to Camp, although not necessarily for the hide-and-seek. "What a delightful invitation! . . . already anticipating the cool breezes of the Adirondacks and the refreshing waters of Spectacle Lake," accepted Liz Carpenter, staff director and press secretary to first lady Mrs. Lady Bird Johnson.[5] Post publicly shared her motivation to invite urban guests to a completely organized retreat, in a natural setting. "I am glad you and your wife evidently enjoyed Betty Beale's article about Camp Topridge," wrote Post to a reader in Illinois, "the fact that I am able to share this with my friends is a source of the greatest pleasure to me and I find great joy in being able to afford busy people the opportunity of a little rest and relaxation away from the intense heat of the Washington summer and the busy, hectic activity of the Capitol."[6] She elaborated, "I like a smoothly running organization and have been blessed with a staff who take pride and pleasure in seeing to it that it is just that. We work out our details meticulously so that matters progress smoothly and this seems to make a very great impression . . . that has always been our way."[7] Regardless of place, Post and staff operated in the same manner.

Invitations to guests started simply with "Hoping so much to find you free to come to Camp Topridge for a little visit . . . the *Merriweather* [Post's private turboprop jet] will take you up and bring you back."[8] These little visits were typically "house parties" for guests that arrived Thursday for evening cocktails and departed mid-Monday morning. Guests received information about appropriate clothing,

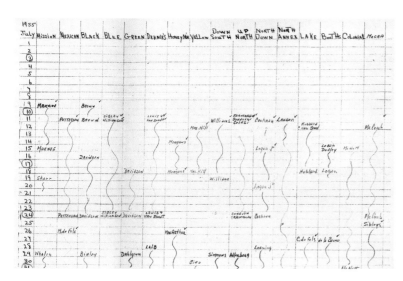

Guest accommodations for 1955 season

"Camp Topridge wants its guests to be as active as you like or as lazy as you like."[9] Invitees could boat, fish, golf at a nearby club, or putt at Camp, swim, play tennis, or hike. Evening attire required dinner and cocktail dresses for the ladies and black tie for the gentlemen, as well as comfortable square-dancing costumes. And a last practical tip, "Camp can be very warm or cool, so be sure and bring sweaters, wraps and a coat."[10] Post's confirmation letters informed guests of the *Merriweather*'s sharp departure time and that lunch would be served on board. She had three requests: that guests arrive early—ten or fifteen minutes before departure; that they kindly have bags "clearly marked with your name to facilitate handling; and PLEASE—NO PRESENTS."[11]

On over 100 acres with frontage on Upper St. Regis Lake, as well as Upper and Lower Spectacle Ponds in New York, Topridge was among the largest and best appointed of "the great Adirondack camps," elegant estates tucked into the area's stunning natural beauty.[12] "And of course the weather was just wonderful compared to [hot, humid] Washington before air conditioning," explained guest Walter Beach.[13] "To run the hotel," as Post put it to a friend, she arrived at Camp in early July just as the painting and opening crew were wrapping up their duties to uncover windows, furniture, and prepare boats with names such as *Dash, Deen-Wee, Pep, Drudge,* and *Merriweather*— which they started to do in May.[14]

"I was so impressed coming here that first time. It opened a whole new world," said staff member Lawrence Lester.[15] Except for maybe six years away from Camp, he stayed on for forty years, working for Post and subsequent owners, eventually becoming caretaker. "This was the biggest camp on the lake . . . it was something you could always tell your friends—I worked at Camp Topridge," said Lawrence, "Carpenters, painters, plumbers, guides worked here . . . Mrs. Post did very well in that area for local people."[16] Locals worked seasonally or year around at Camp, with Post's roving employees (personal maids, social secretary) joining them for Topridge's season that started in July and ended around Labor Day.

Topridge included accommodation for 105 people, guests and staff, in twenty-three separate structures. "We had an 11-room dormitory for the chambermaids . . .

Staff accommodations

Staff cabin

another three-story building (more maids, laundresses, and guides) . . . and then a men's building (for footmen)," explained Lawrence.[17] Others, such as the butler, caretaker, steward, and social secretary had separate cabins. Employees worked in two divisions—the inside staff of maids, butlers, and cooks under steward Frank Moffat, and the outside staff that looked after the grounds, boats, tennis courts, and putting green. Outside staff reported to the caretaker, Ed Russell.[18]

"Always one of my favorite parts of arriving at Camp was that smell of the Adirondacks, pine, spruce and all those wonderful evergreens. That was so special," described granddaughter Ellen.[19] "Any everything, every detail was so well taken care of, the timing of the airplane, the boat,"
recalled guest Julio Heurtematte.[20] To keep everyone on plan, Post, employees, and guests used typed memos and a sixty-line capacity telephone system. "It was like a well-oiled machine: we had our list of guest arrivals and room assignments so when we returned from the airport the maids were waiting to unpack the guests' many suitcases," explained Lawrence.[21] Staff drove limousines and cars to pick guests up from the *Merriweather* airplane and take them to Upper St. Regis landing. With family friends and Washington dignitaries arriving, the staff could be heard saying, "Mr. Ambassador, Mr. Senator," or when in doubt, "sir or ma'am."[22] Young family members would get an official-yet-affectionate "Miss Ellen," for example.[23] Then, Topridge was reached by water. Staff boarded guests onto the

*top*
Camp Topridge boathouse, designed in celebrated Adirondack style

*middle*
Dressed for cocktails

Boathouse cottage porch

*Merriweather* boat for a short ride to the Topridge boathouse, a celebrated example of the Adirondack vernacular style.[24]

This short journey was done in style. Luggage and guests did not travel together. Social columnist Betty Beale explained that the boatmen had uniforms and "even if only one person was going across, two boats [one for the guest, and the other for their luggage] went."[25] In fact, luggage went by a different route, and so suitcases could be distributed to guest rooms before they arrived. Then, chambermaids unpacked the cases and pressed anything that was wrinkled—this was not the era of permanent press fabrics. By the time guests took the funicular (an elevator/gondola carrying them from the boathouse up the hill), enjoyed the tea waiting for them, and were shown to their domain for the long weekend, their clothes were laid out for them.[26] Betty Beale laughed that because returning guests knew the staff would handle their clothes, "of course you wanted to take your best of everything."[27] The over fifteen well-appointed guest and family spaces included one or two bedrooms, sleeping porch, and/or sitting rooms. Some were decorated according to particular themes, such as "Mission" or "Mexican," while others featured contemporary décor.[28]

"Life was so orderly [under Marjorie Post], always," remarked guest Walter Beach.[29] A memo for guests inside the cabin indicated the meal and event schedule for the weekend, with the first order of business being cocktails in "the big room" at 7 p.m.[30] Properly attired after having their clothes and shoes pressed and polished, guests in black tie, dinner dresses, and jewelry enjoyed cocktails in

Detail, boathouse cottage porch

"It was like a well-oiled machine: we had our list of guest arrivals and room assignments so when we returned from the airport the maids were waiting to unpack the guests' many suitcases..."

*above*    Marjorie Merriweather Post's Camp Topridge cabin
*left*      Bathmat from Post's era at Camp

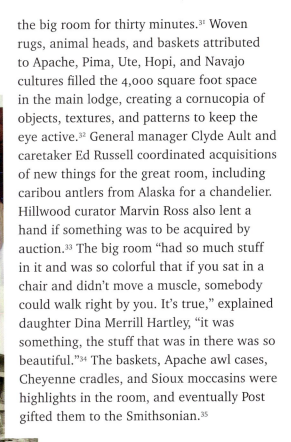

*top right*
Guests Sadie and Major General H. Conger Pratt

*right*
Main lodge, Camp Topridge

the big room for thirty minutes.[31] Woven rugs, animal heads, and baskets attributed to Apache, Pima, Ute, Hopi, and Navajo cultures filled the 4,000 square foot space in the main lodge, creating a cornucopia of objects, textures, and patterns to keep the eye active.[32] General manager Clyde Ault and caretaker Ed Russell coordinated acquisitions of new things for the great room, including caribou antlers from Alaska for a chandelier. Hillwood curator Marvin Ross also lent a hand if something was to be acquired by auction.[33] The big room "had so much stuff in it and was so colorful that if you sat in a chair and didn't move a muscle, somebody could walk right by you. It's true," explained daughter Dina Merrill Hartley, "it was something, the stuff that was in there was so beautiful."[34] The baskets, Apache awl cases, Cheyenne cradles, and Sioux moccasins were highlights in the room, and eventually Post gifted them to the Smithsonian.[35]

The Big Room featuring a cornucopia of objects, Camp Topridge

*top*     Detail, bark wallpaper in Camp dining room
*middle*   Dining service, Camp Topridge
*bottom*   Post and guests at dinner, Camp Topridge

Camp Topridge menu, 1968

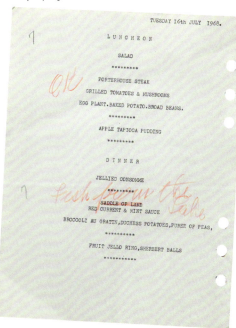

"Of course at dinner we were dressed with tuxedos, formal, even in the middle of the mountains," described guest Walter Beach.[36] Around the table, footmen in tie, jacket, and cummerbund served dinner onto Copeland, Staffordshire, and Franciscan services.[37] Three cooks worked in the kitchen, plus two or more kitchen assistants. Post reviewed each menu, which consisted of finely prepared American cooking with a few foreign-inspired dishes, initialing her approval, or marking changes. One dinner started with chicken soup, followed by roast beef, Yorkshire pudding, green beans, cauliflower, mashed potatoes, and blueberry cheesecake for dessert. Other 1966, 1968, and 1971 starters at Camp consisted of chicken and rice soup, jellied consommé, caviar with blinis, carrot vichyssoise, or melon. And main courses included filet of beef with béarnaise sauce, saddle of lamb, duckling with apple sauce, baked ham, roast

*opposite*
Dacha, Camp Topridge

*right*
Round-and-square band, 1968

*bottom right*
Post and dance instructor, 1968

capon, or porterhouse steak. Vegetables such as asparagus, broccoli, duchess potatoes, green beans, peas and onions, or squash accompanied meals. With local berries and Post's director emerita role at General Foods, a fruit Jell-O ring with sherbet, blueberry pudding, as well as chocolate mousse, charlotte russe, or pineapple delight completed Camp dinners.[38]

Marjorie Post and guests that had them then wore proper square-dancing outfits for the 9 p.m. "round-and-square" (round for ballroom) dance held at Camp's dacha building. Professional Arthur Murray dancers from nearby Saranac instructed guests and filled in when a spare man or lady was needed. In August 1969, dancers Federico MacMaster, Frank Benham, and Statia Mark kept the "do-sa-do" and "slow, slow, quick quick slow" steps flowing.[39] Grandson Stanley Rumbough remembered, "Grandmother would enjoy doing fancy dances, one was the *paso doble* . . . she was amazingly agile on her feet and she'd do it with great flair . . . she did that and the tango and waltz—those were her three favorites. The square dances were more for the guests and kids."[40] The first evening of the Camp Topridge house party concluded with everyone returning to their cabins. "I will never forget falling asleep at night listening to the sound of the loons, the water lapping against the shore and the wind whistling through the pine trees," described daughter Dina Merrill Hartley.[41]

The first meal of the day was just a telephone call away. "Breakfast was wherever you wanted it," expressed guest Julio Heurtematte with fondness, "the staff would bring you this incredible breakfast tray—and I say, I aspire to the tray life."[42] Granddaughter Ellen Charles expanded, "Anything you could dream up for breakfast you could have."[43] Pancakes, sausage, eggs, toast—whatever the selection—breakfast was brought to guests in covered dishes, or guests could eat in the breakfast room of the main lodge. Post took hers in her cabin. Furthermore, "You didn't have to have [General Foods' founding product, the coffee substitute] Postum," continued Ellen, "I didn't drink it. I tried it a couple of times but it was a taste I could never acquire."[44] Although not required fare, the staff made sure General Foods products such as Post Toasties and Grape Nuts were on hand for breakfast. When Topridge caretaker Ed Russell informed the local supermarket that they didn't carry any Post cereals, the grocer changed what they stocked. The cereals continue to be popular in the region to this day. On any given day at Topridge during the season, approximately 100 people (family, guests, and staff) could be taking breakfast, lunch, and dinner. Not surprisingly, given the volume of meals that had to be prepared and the fact that Marjorie Post owned Birds Eye, Camp was equipped with a bank of freezers.[45]

Unlike a garden tea or dinner party at Hillwood where all guests shared in the same activity, mornings and afternoons at Camp offered many informal options from which to pick and choose. "THE CARDINAL RULE AT TOPRIDGE IS: DON'T DO ANYTHING YOU DON'T WANT TO DO. AND IF YOU NEED OR WANT SOMETHING PLEASE ASK," established Post's welcome memo that listed the many amenities of Topridge.[46] "You will find the beach on Upper Spectacle Lake, complete with chairs to sun in," explained the memo, "in the little boathouse, there are boats and canoes on Upper Spectacle Lake, [and] in the big boathouse on Upper Regis Lake, there are canoes."[47] Rackets and balls awaited guests at Topridge's tennis court, ping-pong was ready for players in the small tennis house, and a shuffleboard game or putting green practice was just steps away. Trekking through the woods was yet another option. From Camp there was an established two-mile trail around Upper Spectacle Lake, a longer hike around Lower Spectacle Lake, as well as a two-hour walk that included, according to the memo, a "magnificent view from the top of St. Regis Mountain—100 lakes."[48]

*above*
Big Room, 1968

*right*
Impromptu hula lesson, Topridge tennis court

Yet it was not just the delightful drop-in outdoor offerings that made Camp a favorite of family, friends, and high-powered Washingtonians taking respite—it was the ample assistance of Topridge staff. "If you want a motor boat to take you across the lake or just for a ride, call the operator #158 and boat and boatmen will be arranged for you, there is a lovely [one-hour trip where] you will get a good view of all the camps on the lakes," encouraged the memo.[49] Likewise for golf, calling the operator would set in motion preparations at the Saranac Inn or Lake Placid Club courses. Spottswood P. Dudley, a young guest at the time, recalled the experience of calling for water-skiing arrangements:

> You met three guides in green uniforms sitting in the most beautiful Criss-Craft you've ever seen in your life with a ski rope in their hands. Not seeing any skis I

Topridge guest enjoys motor boating

asked what choices I might have. At that moment they pulled back a sliding door where there must have been fourteen pairs of brand new skis. Selecting a slalom ski, I was quickly off roaring across the lake. It was hard at that moment not to feel like you were the playboy of the western world. Until you realized after about fifteen or twenty minutes you couldn't ski anymore, you're too tired. So you'd let go of the rope. And the boat would come around and the three of them would look at you and say, "Well, tell us when you're ready to go again." I quickly asked if one of them would take a turn.[50]

Likewise, shopping in Lake Placid or attending Catholic, Presbyterian, or Episcopal services was a matter of calling the operator and asking for a boat and a car to take you there. Staff was there to attend completely to guests'

needs and desires: there was even an on-site masseur.[51] Spottswood continued,

I came in from water skiing and my back was hurting. Mrs. Post was walking down the path and she saw me going by and she said, what's the matter with you? I said, "I think I pulled a muscle in my back." She said, "Well you go see Mr. Hand." I said, "Who's Mr. Hand?" Well, who in the world would have a masseur named Joe Hand? Nobody but Mrs. Post! So you'd go in to see Joe and Joe worked it out for me . . . it was hard to go back to normal summer camp after being at Camp Topridge.[52]

Topridge offered perfect days of fishing, "They must have had people with scuba tanks on underneath because as soon as you put your hook down somebody gave you a fish, it was just that good," exclaimed Spottswood.[53] Granddaughter Ellen Charles reflected, "I've always felt it was the best way to fish—you went out with a guide who baited your hook."[54] Fishing was a favorite not only with young guests and family members, but with staff. They would go together. Ellen explained, "Marvin Ross was the first curator at Hillwood and he loved to fish, we would go out in the mornings and row along. I had a little dog I used to take with me and we loved it."[55] Spottswood Dudley added that social secretary Margaret Voigt loved to fish, "She had a vest with hooks on it and would take me under her wing."[56] They fished together with Margaret encouragingly saying to Spottswood he was a great fisherman. Sometimes the guides and kitchen arranged to have guests' fresh catches cooked for breakfast, lunch, or dinner. "If it was particularly good

# "I have some great memories of her . . . I remember the day on the putting green she won my $5-a-week allowance from me."

fishing, it was because [grandmother] stocked the lake," explained Ellen.[57] Although Margaret had a hand in coordinating how much and what kind of fish to stock, she kindly never revealed this to enthusiastic and accomplished fishermen guests. "Mrs. Post had the most wonderful staff, who were in their own right wonderful people," reflected Spottswood, "for children they quickly became your friend."[58] When Post's grandchildren became adults they would spend time at Camp when house party season was over, enjoying time with their family and visiting with the staff that befriended them as they grew up.

With school schedules, it was easier for grandchildren to visit Camp in summertime than Hillwood in spring and autumn. "We would arrive, go up to our cabins and the word would be 'Your grandmother wants to see you,' so we would go to her cabin and be briefed about what was going to happen," explained granddaughter Ellen Charles, "I often went to see her in the morning when she was getting ready for the day—she'd have wonderful stories to tell about her memories at Camp and wanted to know what we were doing."[59] Sometimes the young people in nearby camps would meet for tennis tournaments and round robins. And there were private backgammon lessons and matches, as Ellen described:

> My sister and I were taught to play backgammon by grandmother and she was really tough. She had high standards and after you played for a while you were no longer allowed to count, you had to know. I mean, just her aura made you forget, but she always won. As life went on and we got a little better sometimes we'd beat her and then she wouldn't play with you anymore. She was a good backgammon player and she was a demanding, but excellent teacher.[60]

Young guest Spottswood Dudley also recalled the high stakes of game playing with Marjorie Post, "I have some great memories of her . . . I remember the day on the putting green she won my $5-a-week allowance from me."[61]

Grandchildren also found their own ways of enjoying the natural setting of the Adirondacks. Grandson Stanley Rumbough remembered: "Mommyda [the name some of the grandchildren called Post] had this wonderful pewter pitcher, which I now have, one of my prized possessions, and it used to be full of peanuts—so we would feed the chipmunks."[62] Daughter Dina Merrill Hartley and granddaughter Nina Rumbough hunted frogs. "I was a very good frog catcher. I used to sneak up behind them bare-handed," recalled Dina.[63] "Sometimes you'd go out at night and you used a flashlight and you'd find them … but I remember this champion frog-catcher [my mother Dina Merrill Hartley] beating me," laughed Nina with fondness.[64] Along with the fresh catch from the lake appearing on Topridge menus, so did frog legs, which were served in July 1968 accompanied by zucchini, scalloped potatoes, wax beans, and snow pudding for dessert.[65] Perhaps a coincidence or not, on one occasion Mommyda mentioned that her pet frog had disappeared, a large frog whose back she used to go down and tickle. "That wasn't too good," recalled Nina.[66]

The first lunch bell rang at 1 p.m., followed by the second and final bell at 1:15 p.m. "One thing Mrs. Post did want was promptness at the meal time," said Lawrence Lester, "everyone had to be at their place at the proper time. First bell was the warning; second bell was to be in your seat at the big dining room table."[67] Aside from good manners, there were two other reasons why Post insisted on guests being on time: first, meals were served in courses, not buffet-style, so timing with the cook, servers, and guests was important; second, for housekeeping purposes, staff needed times when they knew guests would not be in their rooms. The forty-six fireplaces at Topridge were checked during lunch and dinner, coordinated by meal bells. "That was one of the things that Mrs. Post looked out for us," explained Lawrence, "at 1:15 p.m. and 7:15 p.m. we knew the guests were out."[68] Outside staff had five or six fireplaces in their purview, with Lawrence assigned to Post's personal cabin:

Post swings golf club at Topridge

> I'd go up there and sit there for five or ten minutes prior to the second bell. When we got the buzz from [maid] Eva upstairs, it would mean that Mrs. Post had just left and we'd get upstairs and start cleaning. And we would take our shoes off and I'd set my fireplaces and get out of there so they could continue so we wouldn't leave ash or dust anywhere. That was precision.[69]

Meanwhile guests enjoyed their lunch with a starter, main course with side, and finished with dessert. For example, salad, followed by breast of chicken with vegetables, then completed with fruit Jell-O. Other lunches started with aspic salad, melon with ham, or mango salad and continued with filet of beef, chicken chow mein, roast beef hash, porterhouse steak, or broiled swordfish. Banana pancakes, cheese, apple pie, and whole wheat bread and butter pudding ended lunchtime menus.[70] Staff had lunch at noon, prepared by their own cook and kitchen maids that attended to three meals a day for employees. After lunch, guests continued with relaxation or activities until dinner. Often Post enjoyed golf.[71]

For evening entertainment there were regular movie screenings "for the lake."[72] Owners of nearby camps and their guests were invited to join Post and her guests at Topridge to take in what was often a first-run film. Topridge "was the one big place, it was the hub of entertainment and activity of all the lakes here, and we were always cordially invited to go to the movies, the employees," added Lawrence Lester.[73] The film schedule was posted at the shared boat landing used by all camp owners in the area.

While Topridge guests ate dinner at 7:15 p.m., two housemen and a parlor maid set up the big room for the 9 p.m. screening. Drawn drapes separated the diners from the bustle in the big room. Large furnishings were moved against the walls and the movie-night chairs were brought up from downstairs storage and placed auditorium-style around the screen. Grandson Stanley Rumbough fondly remembered how the neighborhood cinema-goers arrived via water:

All the [lake] guests would arrive during our dessert. The boatmen would be down below and there were so many people coming in their boats that they'd be rafting them. They'd have one boat at the dock and then maybe two tied up on the outside. Everybody was very polite. Mommyda would come in and they would all stand up, almost in unison saying, "Good evening, Mrs. Post." And then some of the older people would come by and make their pleasantries. And then we'd all sit down and watch the movie.[74]

With Topridge guests, nearby owners, and staff seated Post took her station outfitted with a buzzer and telephone. From there she called professional projectionist Frank Kawatch in the balcony to start the film, later adding requests to adjust the sound or picture. Frank welcomed young visitors in the balcony who wanted to watch from there, or to see the set-up for widescreen and Cinemascope. However, the proper theater equipment from New York and Washington, D.C. suppliers did not detract from the rustic setting.[75] "Mommyda would wear a scarf on her head because the bat would fly around during movies," said Nina Rumbough.[76]

Film projector, Camp Topridge

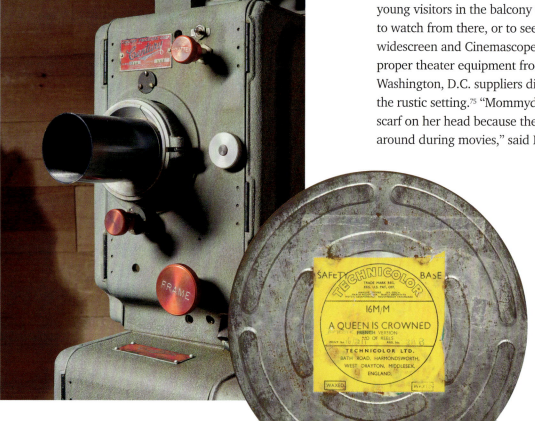

Film canister, Camp Topridge, 1953

After watching Richard Burton as Henry VIII in *Anne of the Thousand Days*, George C. Scott and Joanne Woodward in *They Might Be Giants*, *Flipper's New Adventure*, or Kurt Russell in *The Horse in the Gray Flannel Suit* guests turned in to their cabins or departed for neighboring camps around 11 p.m. Two staff members couriered the three to four film canisters via boat to the switch point, where at 5 a.m. they would be picked up and a new film dropped off. "If you did that, it would be midnight before you got home and got to go to sleep but it never bothered anybody because everyone was enjoying it," recalled Lawrence.[77]

One daytime group outing was the "carry." "Grandmother had traditions wherever she was, especially for the Adirondacks because that was very much a family occasion for the summer," detailed Ellen Charles.[78] The carry was not a requirement, but nearly everyone joined in for the day-long experience of canoeing in beautifully crafted Adirondack guide boats, and then carrying the gear across land to the next water launch point, eventually stopping to picnic. The day included five land carries, with guests responsible for the picnic supplies and staff for the sixty-five pound guide boats, which they lifted over their heads with the oars and seats tied down with rope. Lawrence Lester described the early part of the day, starting with preparing the food at 8 a.m.:

> That consisted always of the same fare: shell steak for the meat and fried potatoes, and sometimes canned peas and carrots, then pancake batter, maple syrup, maple sugar and butter—that was what the picnic food consisted of—and Maxwell House coffee, part of General

*top*
Topridge staff carrying gear to the next launch point

*bottom*
Camp guests enjoying a carry

opposite
Topridge staff cooking the carry picnic

Ferns border picnic blanket at carry lunch

## "Then grandmother would say, 'Now we're going to collect ferns,' and we would decorate the edge of the tablecloth."

Foods, it was good coffee too. We carried our charcoal to do the meat and the potatoes. Then we would get our guide boats into Bog Pond and we would wait for Mrs. Post's guests, who would come by powerboat. We had two guests in each guide boat, so there were three of us with the guide and two guests . . . Mrs. Post would tell the guests that they would be expected to carry the pack baskets and the frying pans and the coffee pot. Once we arrived at the picnic scene we had an oilcloth that we laid on the ground."[79]

Ellen Charles continued, "Then grandmother would say, 'Now we're going to collect ferns,' and we would decorate the edge of the tablecloth with the ferns."[80] After the wonderful hot meal, "Mom would stir up the batter for the pancakes," remembered daughter Dina Merrill Hartley, "she would make the flapjacks and flip them over."[81] The twelve inch pancakes would then be assembled in layers with crunchy maple sugar, syrup, and butter then sliced into

Aerial view of Camp Topridge

cake-like pieces. "It was truly delicious and you always had that once during your stay at Camp—that was tradition," explained Ellen.[82] There would be a rest, then repacking for the return journey to Topridge, with guests and staff back around 5 p.m.

By mid-morning Monday, after another delightful made-to-order breakfast, it was time for the house party to end, with Washington, D.C. guests leaving Camp at 10 a.m. for the airport, where the *Merriweather* jet awaited to take them back to the District. Working around Post's direct instruction not to bring gifts, guests became creative as they could not leave without expressing their gratitude. John Alden Brown wrote a poem ending with:

> Can't help but love the hostess
> Whose every thought and task
> Is to make you happy and it's your fault if you don't ask
> Mix them all together, and you get a little smidge
> Of the happiness we all find at Camp Topridge[83]

As granddaughter Ellen Charles so aptly summed it up, "Everything was so perfect [at Topridge], it was really hard to re-enter the real world when you got home, but it was a wonderful experience and a beautiful, beautiful spot."[84]

"Everything was so perfect [at Topridge], it was really hard to re-enter the real world when you got home..."

# PRIVATE HILLWOOD

## Autumn

Aerial view of Hillwood showing the Lunar Lawn and Japanese-style garden

In autumn, Marjorie Post and her roving staff returned to Hillwood. As in spring, Washington social events took place at the estate, but the gardens were now filled with chrysanthemums instead of tulips. Despite many newspaper articles covering events at Hillwood, there was a private side to running the estate. Six security personnel on rotating shifts looked after Post and her property.[1] The inside staff at Hillwood numbered sixteen to eighteen including the butler, footmen, and maids who received housing and meals as part of their compensation. Some, such as Mr. Gus, chose to live off the estate. He kept an apartment on nearby Porter Street for nineteen years at his own cost.[2] Outside staff, such as the 12–15 gardeners, generally did not live at the estate—but there were occasional exceptions over the years.[3]

Post started renovations to Hillwood in 1955, with the estate fully operational by 1957. Financial manager Donald Handelman, whom Post hand-picked to help with the project management, remembered: "I don't think that there were, at that time, many pieces of property, if any, the size of this that required the staff that we had. This was just her domestic staff to run the property."[4] Post wanted housing for the butler, Mr. Taylor (Mr. Gus's predecessor), McRae, the groundsperson at the time, and the chauffeurs among other staff accommodations. Her memos to architect Alexander McIlvaine stated:

> Staff Rooms to be larger . . . staff dining, large enough for one end to be a sitting room. Back entrance door not to be into kitchen but into hall, with coat closets adjacent, receiving room and flower room.

*below*    Staff outbuildings, including men's dormitory on right
*middle*   Staff dining room and lounge
*bottom*   Hillwood kitchen staff, 1958

Modern equipment in kitchen and pantry, with good table linen cupboard and silver safe . . . dumb waiter to silver safe in cellar. Since we seem to have been able to have various Staff Rooms in the house, it will relieve the situation in the outer buildings, which is very useful as it is much nicer for the maids to be in the house instead of having to go outdoors to their quarters.[5]

Post took genuine pleasure in designing homes to suit her needs, telling Donald Handelman something along the lines of, "I want to make some minor modifications and renovations to the house. Nothing major. This is my plan."[6]

Outbuildings on the estate—separate structures not attached to the mansion—included a chauffeur's house with garage, house for the steward, unmarried male staff dormitory, and gardener's house. They were built in brick, in keeping with the style and size of 1950s suburban homes. For staff bedrooms in the mansion, men's dormitory, and chauffeurs' quarters in particular, Post provided furniture. Matching bedroom suites with a single bed, two night tables, dresser, a writing table, and chairs in bleached wood, painted wood, and French-carved wood are inventoried staff furnishings, along with individual pieces in mahogany and maple accompanied by glass, china, or brass lamps. Broadloom carpets, oriental-patterned rugs, and linen drapes covered the floors and windows. The staff sitting room included a Zenith portable television, yellow curtains, flower vases, smoking accessories, and nature paintings. Keeping to Post's instructions, the remodeled kitchen and butler's pantry was modern, with glass-front metal cabinets

*right* Garden staff planting tulip bulbs
*below* Staff dining room and lounge

*opposite* Marjorie Post and head gardener Earl Loy in Hillwood gardens

in yellow or green and stainless steel work surfaces. Electrical appliances included stainless steel refrigerators by Koch, a Sunbeam mixmaster, four-slice Toastmaster, Kitchen-Cud electric masher, and an electric plate.[7]

Earl Loy spent thirty-five years working for Marjorie Post, having started at Tregaron, her Washington, D.C. residence prior to Hillwood. When she and Joseph Davies divorced, Earl stayed on with her to become head gardener. His day started at 7 a.m. Three cooks—one focused on the mistress of the house and the other two on staff—prepared three meals a day. The staff had breakfast with ham and eggs, or bacon in the staff dining room at 8 a.m. Soon after, Earl began arranging flowers to accompany Post's breakfast, "flowers on that breakfast tray every morning . . . I always fixed up orchids [or some other blooms]."[8] Until it was time for lunch, Post spent the morning in her dressing room, which was set up for light exercises and stretches, grooming, and business meetings with staff and consultants. At 9:30 a.m. Earl met with Post in the dressing room regarding the gardens. He recalled that

she would be combing her hair . . . and a lot of times I'd tell Eva, the personal maid, "I can't go in there. She's not dressed." And then she'd say, "Earl, is that you? Come on in." And she would, you know, have her slip on. Sometimes she was funny, she would write a note, and like myself, she wasn't the best writer in the world. But she would say, "Read it back to me." And [I said], "I'm sorry, I can't read it back to you." And she was giggling, and she'd say, "Well, I can't read it either," and would tear it up.[9]

Inside the mansion, the garden staff maintained plants in the entry hall, as well as orchids and ferns in the breakfast room. Fresh flower arrangements lasted about two days, with absolutely no dead flowers on display in the house. Post occasionally tweaked an arrangement by taking out one stem. And outdoors garden staff maintained narcissus, pansies, tulips, azaleas, Jacob's ladder, rhododendrons, roses, and aucuba among many other plants.[10]

About 10 a.m. employees took a hot bun and coffee break, and the head of the household was ready for breakfast in her dressing room. Eva Zackrisson, the first of two personal maids, called down to the butler's pantry with her breakfast order. Sometimes that included a soft boiled egg but, as butler Mr. Gus explained,

*opposite* Staircase

*above* Butler's pantry

*right* Post's favorites for breakfast including banana, Grape Nuts, tea, and toast

Breakfast room with orchids, 1970s

"there was always a banana on the tray, Post Grape Nuts—[in] little boxes—tea, toast, and a finger towel" along with the flower arrangement Earl prepared.[11] When Post had finished, Eva called Mr. Gus to bring up the lunch and dinner menus for the day to see if Post wanted to adjust anything, or let staff know she was having a small number of guests for lunch or dinner.[12]

"Something else she did, she furnished clothes, we [the garden staff] all dressed alike," offered Earl.[13] They wore matching khaki pants and shirt with a black tie and changed to blue pants with jackets in the winter with gloves and boots also provided by Post. The clothing company tailor came to Hillwood to measure the staff, and the estate laundered the uniforms.[14] When meeting with Post, the personal maids, secretaries, steward, and head gardener wore dresses or suits, purchased from an estate clothing allowance.[15] For example, Earl changed from the garden uniform into a suit for his morning meetings in Post's dressing room. Butlers and footmen enjoyed a more "relaxed" approach in that they wore tuxedos with tails all day, in contrast to previous years when they changed dress for each meal, "It was much easier for all of us [and] was very nice," expressed Mr. Gus.[16] Another perk, if you were a maid, was that "you didn't make up your own room, another maid took care of your room," clarified Earl, "Maids were done at 11:30 a.m. and then could go downtown and do whatever they wanted to do."[17]

Post came downstairs for lunch perfectly groomed, "When she came down, you'd think she was going to a ball," said Earl.[18] Occasionally she stopped in the twenty-two person staff dining room with chrome and leatherette dining chairs to see how things were going, sometimes eating something there, but most of the time she took lunch in the breakfast room with social secretary Margaret Voigt or guests.[19] "Generally, she liked to start with a light soup or a piece of fish . . . it was very tasty and beautifully served, but I mean, it wasn't tea and crumpets . . . and the staff ate the same way she did, maybe it wasn't as formally presented, but it was the same food," explained financial secretary Betty Cannella.[20] It was American cooking in Marjorie Post's homes, "She had a French [cook] once," remembered Mr. Gus, "she stayed a month or six weeks" but Post "wasn't too pleased."[21] Betty Cannella and general manager James Mann monitored provision costs. A comparison of grocers in Washington, D.C. showed that in addition to staples such as flour and sugar, Hillwood staff

Putting green

researched prices for filet of beef, turkey, red potatoes, string beans, bananas, Löwenbräu, cigarettes, and Ritz Crackers.[22]

Also, this was a household of the majority shareholder and director emerita of the General Foods Corporation. Post's granddaughter, Ellen Charles, explained: "[Grandmother] loved the meetings, she loved the board. [She] was very conversant about what was going on and the new products and with the earnings. She was very much involved. We always had the trial products. She tried it on everybody who came, not so much dinner but for lunch—she was a good advertiser."[23] Post told people, "Jell-O is a wonderful product, because of course it's used by all levels of income . . . and it's good for all times."[24] She meant it. In the chandeliered breakfast room at Hillwood, some very special lunches featured the latest flavors of Jell-O and General Foods International Coffee.[25]

About 1 p.m. Hillwood and the financial office downtown exchanged mail including marked memos from Post, and staff payroll. When Post was not in residence at Hillwood, all mail went to the financial office and they forwarded correspondence that needed her attention. Plenty of paperwork filtered through her as the proprietress of the estate. In addition to social invitations incoming and outgoing, there were board meeting documents, charitable contributions, staff requests, and insurance matters. Most charitable requests went to the financial office; Betty Cannella advised on past gifts, and Post instructed Betty on the contribution for the year, or for that moment.[26] Post also called Donald Handelman who with his father, Meyer, handled taxes, investments, and other business matters. She used a private line to Meyer and Donald Handelman's office. Post told them, "I don't want to have to go through the switchboard if I want to talk to you. I want you to use this private number if you want to reach me."[27] The telephone number was not used for any other purpose.

Donald remembered the volume of requests, "I was struck by the number of letters she got from people, perfect strangers asking her to put them through school . . . [also] a lot of social friends wanted to do business with her, and one or two may have [but generally] social friends did not see the business side of her."[28] Socially, invitation lists for the May garden parties had to be reviewed. By 1971, there were over 750 addresses and the diplomat guest list included more than twenty-four embassies, which had to be constantly updated with ambassadorial changes. Betty Cannella added, in light of Post's abundant paperwork, it was "because she was so well organized she still had plenty of time for her personal friends and family."[29]

In early afternoon, Post and Earl walked around the gardens to admire their work and discuss adjustments. "She knew the plants," remembered Earl, "she knew exactly what she wanted."[30] From time to time, Post and Earl putted on Hillwood's green. Or sometimes they walked along the back of the estate with Earl bringing her walking shoes purchased at

*opposite* Book bindings by Doris Chips in first-floor library
*below* Japanese-style garden, 1969

Sears Roebuck and Company—a style contrast from her custom dress shoes. When time was not spent with Post, Earl's ongoing work on trees, lawns, and garden paths continued. "I cut the vista down over the Japanese garden. Each man had a section to do. To cut and water," Earl explained.[31] When Post asked Earl why he never refused a task he replied, "Why should I tell you no . . . it's going to be done one way or the other," and she just laughed.[32] Earl's day at Hillwood usually ended at 4 p.m. With the garden staff, they took turns covering the weekends, each working Saturday and Sunday about once a month. Additionally, a painter was on the payroll, since "there is a tremendous amount of continuous work to keep Hillwood in first-class condition, including the iron fencing," wrote Post in 1965.[33] The Hillwood painter also tended to furniture brought from Camp Topridge and Mar-A-Lago.[34]

About every ten days fine book binder Doris Chips met with Post, sometimes for five minutes or just under an hour. Post insisted Doris use the front door into the mansion. "My aunt [Doris] always made note of that, times were much more formal then, my aunt was doing a service and didn't expect a direct meeting—usually intermediaries would be met," recalled nephew Stephen Vanilio.[35] Post and Doris agreed to hand tooling (not machine) and twenty-three carat gold (not imitation) for the book bindings. Stephen felt that Post

> respected [my aunt] as an independent woman. Women simply didn't have their own businesses. My aunt was unmarried. I have to remind people today that [it was] very difficult [then] for women to get a mortgage without the signature of a husband. Frequently, unmarried women would be ostracized. And never ever, in twenty years, do I ever remember a negative comment from Hillwood.[36]

Although Doris also had Jackie Kennedy as a client, Post's commissions constituted the greater part of her business—the consistent patronage not only helped with bills, but also allowed Doris to develop her skills in various aspects of book arts, a legacy that continued with Doris's nephew later crafting head-of-state gifts for the White House.[37]

Marjorie Post did take time to appreciate her decorative arts collection at Hillwood, and walked around by herself to appreciate it.[38] She defined her two interests as "the art of eighteenth-century France and that of Imperial Russia—painting, porcelain, glass, jeweled articles, textiles and furniture," and for her, "as the influence of French artists and artisans was very strong in old St. Petersburg and Moscow, it seems quite natural that these two artistic

Curator Marvin Ross and student guests

Pet cemetery

expressions should be brought together."³⁹ Post derived great pleasure from looking at Russian enamels, "The Russian genius in the use of stimulating color is a spiritual quality related to the land itself."⁴⁰

Curator Marvin Ross also worked with the collection displayed in the mansion, proving himself on one occasion in particular to be a truly devoted steward. When a shelf broke in the Russian porcelain room, he rushed to support it in order to protect the porcelain on that shelf and those below it—it was over two hours later that a staff member found him and was able to relieve his shaking arms and hands.⁴¹ With forewords by Post, Marvin published *The Art of Karl Fabergé* in 1965 and *Russian Porcelains* in 1968. Post completed *Notes on Hillwood*, a room-by-room guide to the mansion's first floor, in 1970.

One item Marvin brought to Post's attention, but she rejected, was a diamond dog collar.⁴² The suggestion was not completely out-of-step, as Post's collection included an eighteenth-century French dog bed with rose-colored satin upholstery. Instructions to Scampi's (Post's much-loved miniature schnauzer) caregiver for when Post traveled noted the dog's preferences for food moistened with tomato juice or diluted vegetable consommé (not too sloppy), cottage cheese (loves cheese of any sort), any meat (other than pork or ham), and General Foods' Gaines Meal Dog Food. And that "Scampi loves to be alone when eating." Along with Coco, Lady Patricia, Petite Chow, Rags, and Bobo, Scampi is memorialized in Hillwood's pet cemetery.⁴³

For dinner, Post returned to the breakfast room. Even when she dined with secretary

First-floor library

Margaret Voigt, alone, or with two guests, the table was set for four at all times. When the number of dinner guests was small, after the meal they sat in the first-floor library. Sometimes Post and Margaret went into the first-floor library to chat briefly and then read until it was time to go upstairs.[44] When the youngest of Post's three daughters, actress Dina Merrill, appeared on television, she went into the second-floor library to watch her, but invariably turned on the television set during a commercial break. "There is that damn commercial," Marjorie Post exclaimed with a sense of humor.[45]

Some evenings, by design, were filled with paperwork. "If she did not have guests for dinner, if she was not going out, then she would go to her room and sit down and do her paperwork until it was time to turn the lights out," remembered financial secretary Betty Cannella, "she did her paperwork three mornings and three evenings . . . she took her various board duties seriously and she planned her schedule, whenever possible, around these duties."[46] These included the General Foods Corporation board and other boards. "[Even] before people went around in jet planes, if she was in Palm Beach and there was a monthly meeting [in Manhattan], she would get on that

*below* Popular books in Post's library
*bottom* Television in second-floor library

*previous page*
Post's bedroom

Sign on Post's bedroom door

train and she would come up for the meeting," recalled Betty.⁴⁷

As a board member, Post prepared for the agenda. Charles Mortimer, chairman of General Foods Corporation, remembered that "Marjorie had the most wonderful and instinctive way of putting her finger on an opportunity; and on the other hand, criticizing constructively the quality or the nature of a product."⁴⁸ When the board was considering the acquisition of Good Seasons—a blend of dry spices that turned into salad dressing when shaken in a container with vinegar and oil—Post quieted the group by saying, "Mr. Chairman, may a housekeeper speak?" She explained that she had experimented with "these Good Seasons mixes and they have a great future."⁴⁹ Charles later commented that while Good Seasons was not one of the great General Foods products, it was successful and an excellent money maker, "showing how astute Marjorie is in my opinion, to be able to recognize, even before the case is proven, what can be an excellent commercial opportunity."⁵⁰

With her evening's paperwork completed, and the accordion-folding security grates on the interior of her bedroom windows attached, personal maid Eva Zackrisson helped Post take her hair down part-way. Post added clips to maintain curls and waves while Eva brushed out the loose sections.⁵¹ Then Post retired for the evening, while two security guards remained on

duty through the night patrolling the grounds, walking the house, and sitting in the butler's pantry. "I'm one of those sleepers," admitted Post, "if I don't have eight to nine hours I'm pretty short of a lot of things that I like."[52] She slept longer if the evening went late and she also "liked a little nap in the afternoon."[53] An ornate sign with closing flaps adorned her bedroom door: when closed it featured a decorative pattern, when open it showed the elegantly engraved instruction, "DO NOT DISTURB—RESTING." Gabriele Weinert, a second personal maid to Post in the late 1960s, did not recall using the door signs. Post told the maids or left a note with instructions when to wake her.[54]

Post's personal bathroom in pink, cream, and white kept with the times, Mamie Eisenhower's 1953 inaugural gown consolidating the craze for "First Lady Pink" that coincided with the availability of household and fashion items in "Mamie Pink" and other never-before-offered colors such as yellow and green.[55] It is worth noting, however, that Post's admiration for all things pink is also evident in her decorative arts collection, which she started in the 1920s— long before the national craze for pink in the mid-1950s. In particular she admired the exquisite color of the 1914 Imperial "Pink Egg" by Fabergé, given to her in 1931. And in 1938, a gift of a pink Fabergé clock delighted her.[56] In addition to a Saint-Gobain heated towel rack, Post's bathroom featured a series of call buttons next to the bathtub labeled maid, Voigt,

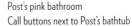

*left*     Post's pink bathroom
*right*    Call buttons next to Post's bathtub

Contents of fallout shelter medical kit, 1967

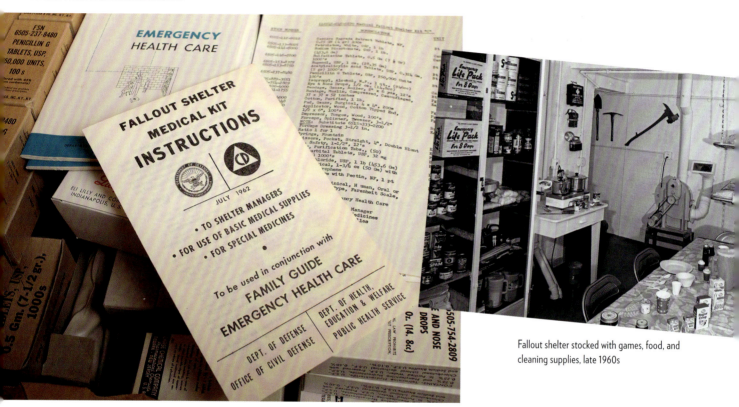

Fallout shelter stocked with games, food, and cleaning supplies, late 1960s

pressing room, sewing room, or door if she needed something from the staff.

In the summer of 1961, general manager Clyde Ault and Post started work on fallout shelters, one in the sub-basement of the mansion, another under the greenhouse, the third near the men's dormitory and the fourth near the chauffeurs' quarters. "Wherever she built them was where the staff would be roughly. I mean [they were] for the staff and all," described head gardener Earl Loy.[57] Combined, the shelters could accommodate sixty-seven people. As historian Stephanie Brown contextualized, Clyde Ault obtained bids just a few weeks after President Kennedy, in July 1961, urged not only city and state governments but "individual Americans" to prepare for potential radioactive fallout.[58] By September 1962, insurance photographs documented the Hillwood shelters stocked with survival kits, General Foods products, and even magazines and games. "The beds and everything and all, they were from the Navy," remembered Earl, "you could unhook them and they would lay against the wall . . . [staff] restocked [food] about every month and a half."[59]

The riots that erupted across the country on the evening of April 4, 1968 with concentrations at Fourteenth and U Street in Washington, D.C. prompted the fabrication of riot shutters for the mansion that covered the windows and French doors of the first floor.[60] Esteemed American historian James Patterson called 1968

Post Toasties and Sugar Crisp cereal set out on fallout shelter table, late 1960s

"the most turbulent year."⁶¹ With the attack on the U.S. embassy in Saigon during the Tet offensive in late January; the assassination of Martin Luther King on April 4; occupations and riots by students and workers in Tokyo, Mexico City, Paris, West Berlin, and New York; visible marches by black, American Indian, and Mexican-American activists; and demonstrations at the Democratic National Convention in Chicago, by September of that year Post felt the tension.⁶² She wrote to the ambassador of Sweden,

> It would seem that the whole world has gone quite mad. In this great Country we are certainly having our problems and goodness knows what will happen about the elections in November. I just cannot understand what it is all about and it is dreadfully disturbing. Sometimes I wish there was a nice quiet little cave I could crawl peacefully into … I am longing to be back at Hillwood. As you know, I did not open the house last Spring because of tensions and upset there, but I missed it very much and am looking forward so much to my return.⁶³

She returned to Washington. By October 1969 Post and staff were hosting Vietnam veterans at Hillwood.

Other improvements in infrastructure and equipment at Hillwood had nothing to do with pivotal changes in American culture. Hairdresser Stewart Bankert remembered that

Cistern for heating and filtering rainwater to wash Post's hair

Massage room, also equipped for hair dressing

at Hillwood, "a special room was set up for our hairdressing. She had a reservoir built on the roof to catch rainwater, [which would] then [flow] into a filtration system and a heating tank. This [heated water] was then piped to the hairdressing room."[64] Post also purchased a spiral permanent wave machine, "as this was the only method that could be used on long hair [at that time]," explained Stewart.[65] Post's thick hair hung below her waist.

About three times a year Stewart permed Post's hair, usually on a Sunday—the day his shop was closed. Their day started at 10 a.m., ending at nearly 7 p.m. "The permanent wave procedure was long . . . I had to be very careful that I didn't apply heat on her hair that had the heat from the previous permanent . . . so it was tricky," admitted Stewart, "the whole darn machine would be so hot."[66] When Stewart suggested, "Wouldn't it be simpler if you would have your hair really just shortened and cut? It's so thick and nice. It would look great," Post responded:

No. I see all these women. They can't go out unless they have an appointment with the beauty shop that afternoon. I can go anytime I want and I don't have to worry. I just take my hair and twist it up and go. Otherwise, I'd have to be going, having it all teased and fluffed up and all—I don't have that much time.[67]

"But she wasn't a person that did as others did," summarized Stewart, "she wanted everything so orderly. I think she felt that hair sticking out wouldn't have suited her at all. She wanted that smooth, trim, sleek appearance."[68]

When Post had time for a manicure, she called Elizabeth Arden's, and Rose Dickens arrived at Hillwood by taxi. Rose described, "In the bedroom there was this table, and on it were all these crowns."[69] And Post invited her to try one on. "I put it on my head, and I looked in the mirror . . . here's this gorgeous crown, and I'm in a nurse's uniform," chuckled Rose, "but that's

# "I put it on my head, and I looked in the mirror... here's this gorgeous crown, and I'm in a nurse's uniform..."

the way she was. She knew I loved her things."[70] When manicure appointments fell over lunch, Rose joined Post. Mr. Gus brought up a tray, and the napkin had a beautiful border. "You know she loved her linens and it was just a masterpiece ... it looked pretty on your lap, but [Marjorie Post] was wise, she had tissues to remove your lipstick," recalled Rose.[71]

Post did not handle cash, so Eva Zackrisson, the personal maid, always paid Rose. One day Eva handed Rose a thick envelope containing a $200 bonus. Post said to Rose, "I just got a tax refund and I want you to have this."[72] Rose explained that Post "had a very down-to-earth warm way of presenting things to make you comfortable ... of course it wasn't a tax refund—that was her humor."[73]

Post sent thank-you telegrams, thinking-of-you letters, and gifts to staff and consultants. "It was really thrilling to arrive home last Sunday and to see the garden looking so perfectly beautiful," she wrote to head gardener Earl Loy.[74] Financial consultant Meyer Handelman replied to Post, "Many, many thanks for your unexpected message ... and your words of praise and appreciation ... we shall do everything in our power to continue to merit your confidence."[75] For Mr. Gus's recovery from surgery she provided three nurses to look after him around the clock.[76] And Post gave specific directions "to send three colors of roses—12 of each" to Meyer Handelman's ailing wife, and,

Russian nuptial crown from Post's collection

Handy tissue booklet for removing lipstick before using fine linen napkins

when the situation was grim, wrote to Meyer, "This is an anxiety for you, I know, and I can well realize the sadness her illness must bring to you, but what comfort your constant care, love and courage must be to her."[77]

In turn, the staffs of the properties, the financial office, as well as long-standing grocers and contractors combined resources to offer Post "a token of our last esteem"—a flagpole for Hillwood featuring "the Commodore's flag" on the yardarm—inspired by her beloved *Sea Cloud* sailing ship, which she had sold in 1953.[78] Names of 100 contributors are noted on plaques around the flagpole's base. Signed as from "officers and crew," Post who was traveling at the time received a telegram from the staff on March 15, 1962, her seventy-fifth birthday, "[We] beg to present to you in honor of this special occasion a flagstaff with yardarm to fly the stars and stripes and house ensign aboard the flag ship Hillwood."[79] Her reply came promptly, "I can't tell you how thrilled I am . . . this is the one important item which has been missing at Hillwood."[80]

Following procedures for any event involving guests—even when the guests were fellow staff members—the staff tracked and made accommodation and transportation arrangements for employees attending the official presentation ceremony on October 20, 1962. On behalf of all the contributors, former security officer Charles Cronk, who worked with Post for fifty years, presented the flagpole and a written scroll to Post saying, "Those of us who have been with the organization for many years will always recall the many kind things you have done . . . your deeds speak far better than anything I can say."[81] Pennsylvania congressman James G. Fulton presented two flags that had flown over the Capitol. Then the U.S. flag and the *Sea Cloud* pennon were ceremoniously hoisted. Afterwards, staff and guests enjoyed tea, champagne, fife-and-drum music performed by teenage boys, and a dance by young ladies in Colonial hoopskirts and wigs. Post was noticeably moved at the event. As a friend described in a note to Post, "I know it was an emotion-packed experience for the mistress of the household . . . [you have] so much to be grateful for in terms of devotion of those who have been looking out [for you] all these years, and the wonderful thing is [you realize] it."[82]

Staff honoring Post with flagpole ceremony on October 20, 1962

# MAR-A-LAGO

## Winter

opposite
Mar-A-Lago's lions and spiral columns

Mar-A-Lago entrance hall

Evening lights at Mar-A-Lago

"I was back at the White House by 3 o'clock from my brief visit to that beautiful never-never land—Mrs. Merriweather's home in Palm Beach," wrote Lady Bird Johnson in *A White House Diary*.[1] The first lady was not alone in her response to Mar-A-Lago. "Nowhere is the Post hospitality more exquisite than at Mar-A-Lago in Palm Beach," reported *Time* magazine in 1967.[2] "As far as fantasies as a young kid, it was an amazing place to visit . . . all the little lamps that looked like crowns," remembered granddaughter Nina Rumbough.[3] "The places Mrs. Post had were so vast, it was easy at Mar-A-Lago to be seen and not heard," explained Spottswood Dudley, a young guest to Palm Beach.[4] Social columnist Betty Beale noted in 1956, "There are some younger fry at Marjorie's mammoth, luxurious Mar-A-Lago but the place is so big I was here for days before I saw one or two of them."[5]

"Mar-A-Lago is difficult to describe or to believe . . . it has all the beauty of a palace and the romance of a stage setting," commented Nettie Leitch Major, a hired writer for Marjorie Post.[6] Inspired by Hispano-Moresque, Spanish, Portuguese, Italian, Moorish, French, and English influences, the estate "is the epitome of Mrs. Post's idea of bringing together various Old World features . . . in harmonious effect," explained Nettie Major in a short guide to the property.[7] Aesthetically, Mar-A-Lago was not out of step with nearby luxury hotel The Breakers which featured a frescoed grand loggia. Described as "modified Spanish, enriched by Italian Renaissance motifs," the vacation spot was hailed as "without doubt one of the most magnificent successful examples of a palatial winter resort hotel" by 1928.[8]

Mar-A-Lago was worthy of the same designation, and yet had a bit more exclusivity as a private residence with under a dozen

*opposite*
First-level cloister

Mar-A-Lago outdoor statues, 1965

guest suites, compared to a hotel with over 400 bedrooms.[9] The venue for regular social dances and charity events, the home fit Marjorie Post's standing as "the unchallenged arbiter of who's who and who isn't during the winter season . . . and the queen bee of Palm Beach," reported Margaret Carroll for *Chicago Today*.[10] Deliberate in layout and fantasy aesthetics for large-scale entertaining, it was possible to visit Mar-A-Lago repeatedly and notice something different each time.

"Other people did not live in a place like Mar-A-Lago. It was fun. As I got older, I was allowed to have houseguests and spring vacation there," recalled daughter and actress Dina Merrill.[11] In 1967, the property that stood between sea and lake, hence the name Mar-A-Lago, was assessed as "one of America's most elaborate twentieth-century mansions . . . [and] since its completion, a center of social life in Palm Beach."[12] Moreover, by this time, Mar-A-Lago was one of the few mansions still held by its original owner.[13] Post did not redecorate or modify Mar-A-Lago in any extensive manner, remaining true to her original 1920s vision for the property.

"I love this house, it's been home, a playground, an occupation, everything to me all my life," said James "Jimmy" Griffin Jr.[14] He was six months old when he started living at Mar-A-Lago. It was the Great Depression when his father accepted the superintendent position that included a cottage on the estate. "He had three children at the time, so it was a great help to him, and steady work for the rest of my father's life," explained Jimmy, "I recall taking the job over from him in 1952."[15] After two years with Jimmy at the helm, his mother, Lillian Griffin, wrote to Marjorie Post, "Junior is a replica of his Dad and also a perfectionist."[16] Jimmy admitted, "You know, I got awful attached to this house. I was very possessive of it. I thought it was mine for many years, I guess." Marjorie Post agreed, "This house is really Jimmy's house, he spends more time here than I do, this is his home."[17]

During the season, early January to nearly the end of February, Mar-A-Lago operated with about seventy-five staff members, roughly half assigned to in-house duties and the rest outside. Forty bedrooms housed maids, valets, kitchen staff, chauffeurs, secretaries, laundresses, and watchmen. Benefits in clothing, meals, and transportation matched those at Hillwood and Camp Topridge, plus an employee parcel of Florida beach. In the late 1960s, Post launched a project to find a

Staff in Mar-A-Lago cutting garden, 1962

way to air-condition Mar-A-Lago's staff wing and other employee quarters without cutting into the walls of her commissioned property, completed in 1927. She was extending her stays in Palm Beach into warmer months, as other seasonal residents and guests did, marked by The Breakers offering a fully air-conditioned hotel and a year-round schedule, instead of the December to April season.[18]

By the late 1960s, craftspeople and Marjorie Post realized that replicating such an estate built in the years 1923–27 would be difficult, due to loss of knowledge in the building arts mainly from the lack of commissions during the modern period. The construction of Mar-A-Lago in the 1920s marked Post as a significant employer, especially since she continued building work during a local economic downturn, hiring local craftsmen, laborers, and suppliers.[19] By the 1960s, Post had a fulltime painter, carpenter, and electrician on staff to maintain the property.[20]

And so as to make her stay even more enjoyable, three gardeners maintained two cutting gardens, while each week the *Merriweather* jet brought blooms and potted plants cultivated in Hillwood's greenhouse, along with the guests. Mar-A-Lago parlor maids arranged the cut flowers. "We did the best we could with the [growing] conditions [at Mar-A-Lago], because this is an awful area for bugs, and she didn't like sprays and things, so we had to be very careful," recalled Jimmy, "we grew huge Hollyhocks, they were gorgeous and put them on each spiral [column] on the patio—she just loved those."[21]

Because the desires and activities of guests varied from day to day, and the needs of the property shifted from year to year, Jimmy was not held to a strict budget, although he ended up spending around the same each year. "We were all trusted employees, all of the estate managers and the butlers," he explained, "they left it to our discretion . . . but I did deal with the general manager to let him know what was going on, so he didn't think I was trying to set up my own little monarchy."[22] Bill payment and accounting was left to the financial office in Washington.[23]

"Of course it was a wonderful time working at this type of household," reminisced Gabriele

"Well, you know, being a young girl and being interested in jewelry, I would put on one ring or a certain pair of [Post's] earrings . . ."

Post's Mar-A-Lago bedroom

Weinert, "I didn't have to make up my room, it was done by the chambermaids for the staff."[24] Staff enjoyed private rooms, not having to share with other employees or the household children, which was common at the time. Gabriele started as one of four kitchen maids at Mar-A-Lago, her duties being to clean and cut the vegetables for staff meals. Then she became second personal maid to Marjorie Post, cleaning and suggesting jewelry, retrieving and returning pieces to the safe, pressing clothes, and looking after schnauzer Scampi. "Well, you know, being a young girl and being interested in jewelry, I would put on one ring or a certain pair of [Post's] earrings," admitted Gabriele with a sense of humor, "[but also] I was having a ball just looking at it."[25] Others felt the vicarious visual pleasure of Post's jewelry. The *Palm Beach Daily News* reported in 1971, "Mrs. Post stole the show . . . what a sight! The amethysts are not as big as hen's eggs, but they try."[26]

Young friends in the neighborhood "wanted to come over and see Mar-A-Lago," recalled grandson Stanley Rumbough, "[We'd] go to Palm Beach for spring break."[27] At Easter, Post

*above*     Amethysts, Cartier, 1950
*right*     Bracelet, David Webb, 1961

Adam guest suite, Mar-A-Lago

Fairy-tale bedroom designed for young Dina Merrill Hartley

(or "Mommyda," as she was affectionately known by several of her grandchildren) had an Easter egg hunt on the patio.[28] Family visits at Thanksgiving and Christmas had the family feast scheduled for 1 p.m. Older family members stayed in Mar-A-Lago's private suites, such as the Adam Room, Spanish, Portuguese, Dutch, or American Rooms, each named after their own interior decor.[29] Yet it was the rooms designed for the infant Dina Merrill Hartley that stood out. The suite included a beehive fireplace with blossoms and leaves in plaster relief and tinted polychrome, a silver bed, squirrel-tailed bedposts, and a rug illustrated with scenes from fairy tales. Granddaughter Nina Rumbough remembered staying in the room designed for her mother, "Mommyda (grandmother) always had these wonderful comforters that were satin on one side and velvet on the other, so you'd wrap yourself up in them and parade around pretending you were a princess."[30] Children, especially boys, enjoyed staying in Mar-A-Lago's tower, seventy-five feet tall, and affording a spectacular view in all directions.[31]

Marjorie Post also invited friends and consultants to Mar-A-Lago to blend a little bit of work with a great deal of luxury, or as a treat including spouses and family members in the invitation. Tony Abate, from the clothing design house of Oldrich Royce, would fly to Mar-A-Lago with his wife. "He'd bring his pink boxes with all the dresses in it to be fitted or whatever—I mean I don't know if he actually ever did any work

"Mommyda (grandmother) always had these wonderful comforters that were satin on one side and velvet on the other, so you'd wrap yourself up in them and parade around pretending you were a princess."

*top*
Beehive fireplace, suite designed for young Dina Merrill Hartley

*middle and bottom*
Spanish guest suites, Mar-A-Lago

Second-level cloister with view of tower

*below*  Detail, sheets for the tower guest rooms, meticulously labeled

*bottom*  Detail, guest sheets embroidered to indicate the bottom

while he was there, but [Post] would offer for them to stay . . . it was free rein of the house," explained Abate's children Maria and Michael.³² Henry Dudley was a family friend and later become Post's estate planner. When an invitation was extended to Mar-A-Lago, his wife told their sons to pack two bags, because they needed to be properly dressed for dinner, quipping "Just wait until you see what they do with your luggage on the way home."³³ Spottswood, Henry's son explained, "The valets repacked your bag for you with everything cleaned [and in tissue paper so nothing wrinkled]. I would arrive home with my mother [happily] rubbing her hands [and declaring] 'no work this week' . . . there was no doubt that on a visit to Mrs. Post you came back looking better than you arrived."³⁴

*top*     Mar-A-Lago dining room
*bottom*   Setting the Mar-A-Lago dining table, 1964
*opposite*  Detail, Mar-A-Lago *pietre dure* dining table

While children typically dined separately from adults, young guest Spottswood Dudley recalled his first time at the grand Mar-A-Lago table:

> [It] was my twelfth birthday, and I remember sitting next to the famous U.S. General [McAuliffe] who said "Nuts" to the Germans [in World War II's Battle of the Bulge]. And I remember my father telling me to get up and make a toast to Mrs. Post, thanking her for allowing me to be there for my birthday. It was an incredible experience to be in her realm . . . the other guests were amazing people, senators, ambassadors, generals, authors, artists, etc. . . . you had more forks going this way and more knives going that way than you could figure out . . . if you'd reach for the wrong utensil your protector's [i.e. footman's] white glove would magically appear and direct you to the right one.[35]

The dining room was inspired by a room in the Chigi Palace in Rome, making use of simulated marble columns, copied frescoes on canvas, Spanish chandeliers, and Venetian chairs. Post had Joseph Urban design the table for the dining room when she commissioned Urban and Marion Wyeth to build Mar-A-Lago.[36]

Staff literally labored to keep the table of yellow marble, lapis lazuli, red jasper, red

stone, white alabaster, black stone, white shell, yellow chalcedony, and green jasper functional.³⁷ Superintendent Jimmy Griffin explained:

> It would take four men to put one section in this table [because] the sections weighed 350–400 pounds apiece. [The table] was gorgeous, and it weighed [as much as] 6.5 tons. It was a major job to set it up. We'd have to know a day ahead if she was going to use it for dinner and how many [guests], to know how many sections to put up, and then again to take it back down [to two ends and middle section].³⁸

In 1969, the School of the Medici Marble Works indicated that it would be impossible to make a duplicate table. By then detailed inlay work on a large scale had become a lost art.³⁹ The table meant a great deal to Post, to the point that it was specifically called out in her will to be moved from Mar-A-Lago into Hillwood's museum collection upon her death.

Even though dinner parties at Post's residences nearly always ran like clockwork, there was one unexpected factor that could delay dinner— Marjorie Post would not sit down to a table of thirteen. If at cocktails it appeared there would be thirteen diners at table, the missing guest would be telephoned, and a local tuxedo- or dinner dress-owning replacement would be found—even if it meant extending the cocktail period of the evening. (Usually it happened for a good reason, such as a delayed flight from Washington, D.C. with a congressman guest.) This was one of Post's superstitious habits to avoid bad luck, along with not wearing opals, never putting a hat on a bed, and having all umbrellas closed before entering the home.⁴⁰

Post demonstrating the tango at charity fundraiser, 1962

"All of her parties were occasions . . . they were big, she rarely had small parties, maybe luncheons with someone or a business associate . . . but almost always, the house was filled with guests," described superintendent Jimmy Griffin, "we'd have dinner for about seventy-five and [then] dancing . . . she got all of Palm Beach square dancing, that was a ritual."⁴¹ All of Palm Beach included Rose Kennedy, who regularly sent Post thank-you notes for gifts, travel souvenirs, and invitations, as well as notes when she noticed Post's family in the newspaper. Post complimented Rose in 1965, "I was just on the point of writing to you to tell you what a joy it was to see you bouncing around . . . I am amazed to learn from your letter that it was the first time you ever square danced." Rose attended Mar-A-Lago square dances thereafter, and charmingly wrote to Post, "I have not had so many attractive dancing partners since I was a debutante."⁴² Granddaughter Nina Rumbough felt,

> Probably my most special memories of her dances were in Mar-A-Lago . . . in my teen

*above* Protectors issued to heel-wearing guests
*right* Package information for heel protectors

years, I would get private lessons from professional dancer Federico MacMaster, and my favorite dance was the paso doble. I remember my grandmother being so great at the tango and always holding the floor when the musicians would take a break from playing. The record player would come on and she always used to demonstrate the tango for everyone. And I got to demonstrate the paso doble and that was special. I loved that whole aspect.⁴³

The *Palm Beach Post* printed, "Mrs. Post looked like a hundred million—for her that's easy—in a dear little peasant blouse . . . as she whirled and dipped," and added, "You go to Mrs. Post's to dance or you stay home."⁴⁴

Superintendent Jimmy Griffin recalled that Post started the dances in the 1950s, holding the event indoors. "That meant while they were eating, we'd have to go and dismantle that living room," he explained.⁴⁵ The rugs were rolled, chairs moved, and then "eleven o'clock, everybody went home, and then we'd have to go in and set that room up again so it was fine in the morning, and that was such a hassle—she realized it," remembered Jimmy.⁴⁶ Next Post and staff tried a portable dance floor on the patio. However, "it didn't have any two level points on it . . . and it's cobblestone, so we had sub-flooring made to fit each area, made in six-foot sections—that had to be brought in and this was a huge floor," said Jimmy.⁴⁷ Then the proper dance floor was put on top and surrounded by a decorative and protective fence, so guests would not fall off the two-foot high platform. Another task was protecting the patio floor made of stones and set into a Spanish-inspired pattern. Spiked heels dented and scratched the polished floor, so Post's staff issued plastic caps to heel-wearing guests.⁴⁸ Jimmy explained,

Every woman that got in got hoofed on her heel . . . a lot of them didn't like it either, and if Mrs. Post saw a lady [with heels she'd tell the staff] 'go over and get the plastic caps' and we'd have to put them on her foot right there. It worked, it didn't dent the floors, they didn't really interfere with their dancing, but it was a job, because you had to have a butler or somebody on the door checking feet."⁴⁹

The same concern for the floor remained if guests were taken on an architectural tour of Mar-A-Lago. When on the patio, women were told to "abandon their spiked heels."⁵⁰ This postscript was added to a charity tea invitation, "Ladies, for the protection of Mrs. Post's beautiful rare rugs and floors, please do not wear steel heels."⁵¹ So devoted was Post to the cause of preserving floors that she even sent the heel caps and a series of plastic runners to the White House in 1964 where Lady Bird Johnson passed them on to the chief usher and curator.⁵² Still, rain canceled dancing on the patio, inspiring Post to add a 200-person pavilion designed by Marion Wyeth in 1962, which she used for dances, lectures, and music performances. This was one of just a handful of additions to the property, along with enclosing a space with glass to create the tent room for dining, and fallout shelters in the basement.⁵³

In Post's living room, Rufus, a nine-month-old lion cub, enjoyed attention from guests attending the 1973 Valentine's tea in support of the Animal Rescue League. Less furry attractions for the charity event at Mar-A-Lago in earlier years included tea, forty tables of bridge in the pavilion, and touring the mansion and gardens for the 400 attendees.⁵⁴ "She loved animals," reminisced Jimmy Griffin, "we had a pet cat that died, and she sent us a condolence card."⁵⁵ With Mar-A-Lago as a venue that received much press attention, requests for use of the mansion or grounds were numerous. For example, Post

Round-and-square dance in Mar-A-Lago pavilion, 1964

*opposite*
Mar-A-Lago living room, 1967

agreed to honorary chairmanship of the World Wildlife Fund charity auction in Palm Beach, and the Good Samaritan Hospital Auxiliary "Christmas Caper" fashion show luncheon. She agreed to the English Speaking Union holding lectures at Mar-A-Lago, the Marine Corps using space for seminars, sketching sessions on the grounds by the Lake Worth Art League, and the Garden Club tour in 1964, responding: "The two hurricanes played havoc with our trees and plantings but I am afraid all of Palm Beach suffered rather badly in this way so perhaps we will all be in the same boat."[56]

In addition to thank-you notes, Post received tokens of appreciation such as a sweater "in a lovely shade of blue, and is so attractive in every way that I shall wear it with the great joy."[57] Only not taking the first "no" as a final answer seemed to ruffle Post's feathers. Requests from charities and social organizations asking her to reconsider received a polite second rejection drafted by staff, but behind-the-scenes Post would write a firm "the answer is no!" to social secretary Margaret Voigt. Post was decisive in these matters, and sometimes she truly wished she could accommodate two requests at once, but the first "no" truly meant it was not possible.[58]

Likewise, correspondence from children received replies. In 1970, this letter arrived at Mar-A-Lago, "Dear Mrs. Post, my name is Maxine Grad . . . [when] we pass your house I make my father slow down because I think its [sic] such a beautiful house . . . your products are great . . . is it true you have tunels [sic] going from your house to the beach?" Post replied with color postcards of Mar-A-Lago and a telephone number, writing, "You do not tell me how old you are but I can imagine that you are a very young Miss. Perhaps [your father] will bring you in one morning about ten thirty to see it. If you will call us on the telephone we would be glad to arrange it. P.S. Yes, we do have a tunnel to the beach."[59] Post also kept the grade A papers by Mrs. Barnes's students, who visited Mar-A-Lago in 1968 and for homework wrote their impressions, including the following: "The house wasn't a house, nor was it a palace it was an empire, an empire conquered . . . it was one person's dream come true; I have been through the White House in Washington, D.C. and I can safely say that I enjoyed this more; the fish ponds looked so cool and refreshing I felt like jumping in; I can try to understand the significance of everything, but I never will be able to fully unless I was a Post."[60]

Gift from Sigma Beta Epsilon fraternity at C.W. Post College

*left*
Post and footman hosting Mar-A-Lago guests

*right*
Feather-wearing Rose Kennedy and Post in tiara, 1968

*opposite*
Set for outdoor Mar-A-Lago dining

"She was a fun lady, and because we were a bunch of young guys laughing and having fun every moment of our lives, we brought that joy to her," reflected John Convery.[61] Post accepted the invitation to be honorary housemother of the Sigma Alpha Epsilon fraternity at C.W. Post College in New York. It was not just a token acceptance. "She took it quite seriously," explained John, one of the fraternity presidents who corresponded with "Mother Marjorie" on a regular basis, updating her on what "her boys" were accomplishing.[62] She received the fraternity pin, attended the initiation of the pledges, and wrote back to the fraternity to thank them for mother's day cards and flowers, replying that she was "so proud of you all and want to send my love to you."[63] She was "a tremendous mentor at all levels [and] was feeding me in a very positive way," reflected brother Michael Tucci, who pursued law and acting (later to be cast as Sonny in the 1978 film *Grease*) with Post's encouragement.[64] As a special treat, the fraternity president and one other brother were guests at Mar-A-Lago for two weeks.

In Palm Beach it was always "boys, cocktails at 7, dinner at 7:30, don't be late boys," Post told John and Michael.[65] "Not only did we square dance, but we had the whole crowd having fun doing a circle dance, with Mother Marjorie," explained John, "and then we would have some great times afterward, we sat and talked with her."[66] For some dinners it was Post, her boys, and other guests seated outside at a table of eight. When one of Michael's favorite dishes was served—lamb chops—Post urged him, "Oh Michael, take another."[67] He remembered they were so delicious, "the food was breathtaking, the freshest of fresh . . . I wanted to take them home."[68] On an outing to the Lion Country Safari, Post wanted to buy some copper bracelets but did not have money on her, so John gave her one hundred dollars. At dinner the loan was repaid. "There was a little card on my place setting there and I think it was a hundred and fifty bucks in there—she gave me a little bonus—that was the best loan I

## "... everybody wanted to be with Mrs. Post—she was the Red Cross Ball."

Post and escort Fred Korth, Red Cross Ball, 1967

Lady Bird Johnson in yellow with Mar-A-Lago staff, 1968

ever made," laughed John.[69] "[She] never said anything nasty about anyone . . . and you saw the way she treated people around the house . . . the ethnic groups that worked for her, everything was okay . . . you heard innuendos at other places but you never heard it at that house," reflected Michael.[70]

A highlight of the visit was the Red Cross Ball. Post arranged for tuxedos and dates, taking Michael to Saks on Worth Avenue and selecting his tuxedo with green and black plaid pants. Her boys joined in the festivities along with her other guests—ambassadors from a number of countries. "I was at the best table," recalled Michael, "everybody wanted to be with Mrs. Post—she was the Red Cross Ball."[71]

Post started the International Gala for the Red Cross in 1957, and by the late 1960s served as a willing mentor to the event chair. "That was a big thing," explained superintendent Jimmy Griffin, "she'd bring all of them [ambassadors] and then they'd go as her guest to the ball, which was the biggest event of the year in Palm Beach."[72] The gala included a procession of ambassadors and their wives escorted by Marines in dress blues, and other attendees in white tie, orders, and jeweled or flowered tiaras. In 1967, the meal was in red and white (the colors of the Red Cross), with dancing planned to favored songs such as "I've Got Rhythm" or "Anything Goes" and "Oklahoma."[73] Second personal maid Gabriele Weinert recalled that Post selected her jewelry according to the occasion and that, for the Red Cross Ball, her most gorgeous pieces were worn.[74]

On her *Merriweather* jet, Post flew ambassadors and spouses from Washington, D.C. to stay at Mar-A-Lago. Or she borrowed the General Foods corporate jet if there was a last-minute travel conflict. Marjorie Post personally hosted the ambassadors of India, Italy, Luxembourg, Nicaragua, Panama, France, Kuwait, Peru, Spain, and the U.S.S.R. Other Palm Beach residents welcomed ambassadorial guests from Greece, Ireland, Japan, Mexico, Netherlands, Portugal, and Sweden over the weekend as well.[75] Before the start of the Red Cross Ball, held at the Palm Beach Towers in 1967, Post sent a telegram to the chair, "I know tonight is going to be a great success and we

Post, belle of the Red Cross Ball, 1968

are all anticipating it with the greatest pleasure . . . I just want to send you this little word of warm appreciation and thanks for the perfectly magnificent job you have done."[76]

In April 1968, accompanied by schnauzer Scampi, Post gave Lady Bird Johnson a warm welcome and tour of Mar-A-Lago, with the first lady staying in the magical childhood suite designed for Dina Merrill Hartley.[77] They discussed designs for horticulture projects in and around the nation's capital. Post was recognized as one of the most knowledgeable contributors to the first lady's project, citing specific plants suitable for climate, aesthetics, and reasonable upkeep in the District.[78] The Christmas before the visit they exchanged thoughtful presents. From Post, a check to the Society for a More Beautiful Capital, and from the first lady, a basket of bread baked at the White House accompanied by peach and pear preserves from the LBJ Ranch—mutually perfect gift solutions to and from ladies with everything.[79] Post's plans for Christmas varied, from Hillwood, to Mar-A-Lago, to traveling, but a few holiday seasons in particular at Mar-A-Lago remained in superintendent Jimmy Griffin's mind:

To Marjorie Post with memories of a fabulous visit — Lady Bird Johnson

Post's record book of gifts received and given, D initial being from when married to J.E. Davies

Post kept bound books with typed lists of gifts sent and received. In 1961 friends and family gave her scarves, flowers, framed photographs, books, and various entertaining items, such as cocktail napkins, paper party hats, and canapé plate. Jeweler Harry Winston sent her a box of cheese. Her return gifts included magazine subscriptions, luxurious panty hose, fruit cakes, wreaths, and season tickets to the symphony. Staff received checks, turkeys with a basket of assorted goodies, perfume, and fruit cake while various charities received donations.[81]

Other thoughtful year-round gestures to staff included silver picture frames for wedding anniversaries, flowers to ailing spouses, additional checks for medical bills, and even a pet dog. "She had long-term employees," explained Jimmy Griffin, "we had gardeners with twenty-five to twenty-eight years of service with her, and a lot of inside staff had been with her thirty to thirty-five years . . . says a lot about her, it was a good organization."[82] It showed. "Being at her properties was access to the best resort and best-run place in the world—nobody knows how to live like she did," reflected guest Spottswood Dudley, "in all honesty, it is a wonderful pleasure to have seen it, a treasure really."[83]

A very good friend of Mrs. Post . . . a lovely refined socialite, fell on bad times, and Mrs. Post brought her into the organization—she was her official buyer, Christmas shopper, did all of her Christmas shopping for her throughout the year in Europe and everywhere. The gifts would start coming way ahead and we'd put them in the secretary's dining room, I'm talking about filling this room with gifts . . . and [the socialite] would come here, wrap them all, address them, and have a list of all of them so Mrs. Post could go over the list and everything. Oh, that happened two or three years in a row.[80]

twenty-five to twenty-eight years of service with her, and a lot of inside staff had been with her thirty to thirty-five years . . . says a lot about her, it was a good organization."

Christmas at Mar-A-Lago

Post and guests enjoying tea at Camp Topridge

# Endnotes

**Introduction**

1. Letter from Fori Nehru, January 19, 1969, Post Family Collection.
2. Nancy Rubin, *American Empress*, pp. 32-37, 87-88, 135-40.
3. Letter from General Foods, February 20, 1962, Post Family Collection.
4. Margaret Jones, "Money: Women Hold 80 P.C. of Big Fortunes," *Boston Globe*, January 30, 1966.
5. Myra MacPherson, "Mrs. Post Serves Tea—for 300," *New York Times*, May 26, 1966.
6. Mrs. Merriweather Post, "Notes on Organization," January 1965, Post Family Collection.
7. Transcript of interview with David Zeitlin, *Life* magazine, 1964, Post Family Collection; Nancy Rubin, *American Empress*, p. 73.
8. Transcript of interview with David Zeitlin, *Life* magazine, 1964, Post Family Collection.
9. Ibid.
10. Emlen Night Davies, "My Journey," pp. 5, 9; Nancy Rubin, *American Empress*, pp. 121, 129, 185-86, 222-23, 252.
11. Stephanie Brown, "Descendants of Charles William Post," p. 1.
12. Ellen Charles Oral History, p. 25.
13. Ibid.
14. James Griffin Jr. Oral History, p. 38.
15. Ibid, p. 10.
16. Dina Merrill Hartley Oral History #1, p. 30.
17. James Griffin Jr. Oral History, p. 53. Gabriele Weinert Oral History, p. 14.
18. Gabriele Weinert Oral History, p. 5.
19. James Griffin Jr. Oral History, p. 17. Betty Cannella Oral History, p. 17.
20. Spottswood P. Dudley Oral History, p. 11.
21. James Griffin Jr. Oral History, pp. 16, 45.
22. Frank Del Monte Oral History, p. 11; Merriweather folder, Post Family Collection.
23. Gabriele Weinert Oral History, p. 5.
24. Frank Del Monte Oral History, pp. 10-13, 16-18; Frank Del Monte Jr, "Mrs. Post's Limo," Hillwood Archives.
25. Michael and Maria Abate Oral History, pp. 30-31. Merriweather folders, Post Family Collection.
26. Rodion Cantacuzene Oral History, pp. 9-10. Walter Beach Oral History #1, p. 26. James Griffin Jr. Oral History, p. 14.
27. Gabriele Weinert Oral History, p. 13. Betty Cannella Oral History, p. 21. Mar-A-Lago folders, Gus Modig folder, Post Family Collection.
28. Donald E. Handelman Oral History, p. 12.
29. Ibid, p. 14.
30. Jennifer Conover Oral History, p. 11. Donald E. Handelman Oral History, pp. 10, 11, 13, 14, 31. Charles Mortimer interview by N. L. Major, August 8, 1965, Post Family Collection. Stewart Bankert Oral History, p. 11.
31. Ibid.
32. Transcript of interview with David Zeitlin, *Life* magazine, 1964, Post Family Collection.
33. Donald E. Handelman Oral History, p. 22.

**Spring**

1. Rodion Cantacuzene Oral History, p. 8.
2. Ibid.
3. Gus Modig Oral History #1, p. 12.
4. Ibid, pp. 25-26.
5. Gus Modig Oral History #2, p. 6.
6. Gus Modig Oral History #3, pp. 6-7.
7. Ibid, p. 6.
8. "A World Unique and Magnificent," *Life*, November 5, 1965; "Mrs. Post Serves Tea—for 300," *New York Times*, May 26, 1966.
9. Gus Modig Oral History #3, p. 27.
10. Suzy, "If Mrs. Post Says Formal it IS Formal," *Miami Herald*, November 21, 1967.
11. Gus Modig Oral History #2, p. 8.
12. Betty Beale Oral History, pp. 22-23.
13. Peggy Brown Oral History, p. 7.
14. Ibid.
15. Gus Modig Oral History #3, p. 3.
16. Suzy, "If Mrs. Post Says Formal it IS Formal," *Miami Herald*, November 21, 1967.
17. Gus Modig Oral History #3, p. 29.
18. Gus Modig Oral History #2, p. 7.
19. Ellen Charles Oral History, pp. 14-17.
20. Suzy, "If Mrs. Post Says Formal it IS Formal," *Miami Herald*, November 21, 1967.
21. Gus Modig Oral History #3, pp. 3, 6.
22. Walter Beach Oral History, p. 26.
23. Household Catalogue No. 22, Movie Equipment, Post Family Collection.
24. Hillwood dinner, Thursday December 10, 1970, Hillwood Museum curator files.
25. Betty Beale Oral History, p. 15.
26. Ibid.
27. Gus Modig Oral History #2, p. 4.
28. Gus Modig Oral History #3, p. 10.
29. Anonymous Oral History, October 5, 1998, p. 12.
30. Amy Ballard Oral History, p. 13.
31. Betty Beale, *Power at Play*, pp. 331-32.
32. Perle Skirvin Mesta, *Perle: My Story*, pp. 5-6.
33. Jacqueline Kennedy Oral History, University of Kentucky, in C. David Heymann, *The Georgetown Ladies Social Club*, p. 117.
34. Betty Beale, *Power at Play*, p. 5.
35. Jewell Fenzi, "Elizabeth Moffat White: An Interview."
36. James Barron, "Evangeline Bruce, 77, Hostess Known for Washington Soirees," *New York Times*, December 14, 1995 and C. David Heymann, *The Georgetown Ladies Social Club*, pp. 72, 116, 181.
37. The Women of General Foods Kitchens, *The General Foods Kitchens Cookbook*, pp. 1, 7. General Foods Kitchens, *Baker's Chocolate and Coconut Favorites*.
38. Scrapbooks 1963, 1970, President, and First Ladies files, Post Family Collection.

39. Ibid.
40. Ibid.
41. Ibid.
42. Ibid.
43. Benefits Held at Hillwood and Kennedy Center folders, Post Family Collection.
44. Dorothy McCardle, "Along With a Gift Mrs. Post Gives a Laundry Lesson," *Washington Post*, November 22, 1966.
45. Jewell Fenzi and Allidi Black, *Democratic Women: An Oral History of the Woman's National Democratic Club*, pp. 19–20.
46. Earl Loy Oral History, pp. 45–46.
47. Peggy Brown Oral History, p. 9.
48. Gus Modig Oral History #2, p. 10.
49. "Perennial Party Blooms into Weekend," *Washington Post*, May 1, 1967.
50. Rodion Cantacuzene Oral History, p. 9.
51. Veterans folder, Post Family Collection.
52. Gus Modig Oral History #2, p. 10.
53. Music for Young America program, March 6, 1959.
54. Donnie Radcliffe, "The Witty Mrs. Post: Belle of Umpteen Symphony Balls," *Washington Star*, November 23, 1969.
55. Dorothy McCardle, "Orchestra Plays Upbeat Evening for Mrs. Post," *Washington Post*, March 16, 1967.
56. Herman Schaden, "Symphony Summer Home to Honor Backer," *Washington Post*, September 28, 1966.
57. Pavilion folder, Post Family Collection.
58. Ellen Charles interview with the author, February 23, 2012.
59. Kennedy Center and Kennedy Family folders, Post Family Collection.
60. Ibid.
61. Ibid.
62. Ibid.
63. Lisa Smith Oral History, p. 1.
64. Ibid, p. 4.
65. "Sorority Sisters' Luxury Weekend," *Life*, May 16, 1960.
66. Lisa Smith Oral History, p. 12.
67. Ibid, p. 8.
68. Ibid, p. 11.
69. Ibid, p. 13.
70. Sigma Alpha Theta folder, Post Family Collection.
71. *Life* magazine folder, Post Family Collection.
72. Ibid.
73. "A World Unique and Magnificent," *Life*, November 5, 1965.
74. *Life* magazine folder, Post Family Collection.
75. Ibid.
76. Ibid.
77. Ibid.
78. Ibid.
79. Earl Loy folder, Post Family Collection.
80. Dorothy McCardle, "Along With a Gift Mrs. Post Gives a Laundry Lesson," *Washington Post*, November 22, 1966.

## Summer

1. Dina Merrill Hartley Oral History #1, p. 31.
2. Memories of Camp Topridge Member Program, 2010, p. 10.
3. Nina Rumbough Oral History, p. 4.
4. Stanley Rumbough Oral History, p. 9.
5. Camp Topridge folders, Post Family Collection; Lady Bird Johnson, *A White House Diary*, p. 14.
6. Camp Topridge folders, Post Family Collection.
7. Ibid.
8. Ibid.
9. Ibid.
10. Ibid.
11. Ibid.
12. Harvey Kaiser, *Great Camps of the Adirondacks*, p. 214. Camp Topridge folder, Executive Directors files, Hillwood.
13. Walter Beach Oral History, p. 14.
14. Camp Topridge folders, Post Family Collection.
15. Lawrence Lester Oral History, p. 2.
16. Ibid, p. 23.
17. Ibid, p. 13.
18. Ibid, p. 25.
19. Memories of Camp Topridge Member Program, 2010, pp. 10, 18.
20. Ibid.
21. Lawrence Lester Oral History, p. 29.
22. Ibid, p. 25.
23. Ibid, p. 30.
24. Harvey Kaiser, *Great Camps of the Adirondacks*, p. 213.
25. Betty Beale Oral History, pp. 9–10.
26. Lawrence Lester Oral History, p. 15.
27. Betty Beale Oral History, pp. 9–10.
28. Camp Topridge folders, Post Family Collection. Photograph Collection, Hillwood Archives.
29. Walter Beach Oral History, p. 15.
30. Camp Topridge folders, Post Family Collection.
31. Ibid.
32. "Camp Topridge Revisited," *Architectural Digest*, June 1999.
33. Camp Topridge folders, Post Family Collection.
34. Dina Merrill Hartley Oral History #1, pp. 30–31.
35. Smithsonian Institution, National Museum of Natural History Collections database.
36. Walter Beach Oral History, p. 13.
37. Kathy and Harlan Crow, Camp Topridge Collection.
38. Ibid.
39. Camp Topridge folders, Post Family Collection.
40. Stanley Rumbough Oral History, p. 9.
41. Nancy Perot Mulford, "Adirondack: Camp Topridge Evolves," Hillwood director clippings files.
42. Memories of Camp Topridge Member Program, 2010, p. 21.
43. Ibid.

44. Ibid.
45. "Camp Topridge Revisited," *Architectural Digest*, June 1999.
46. Camp Topridge folders, Post Family Collection.
47. Ibid.
48. Ibid.
49. Ibid.
50. Spottswood P. Dudley Oral History, pp. 4-5.
51. Camp Topridge folders, Post Family Collection.
52. Spottswood P. Dudley Oral History, pp. 5-6, 10.
53. Ibid, p. 5.
54. Memories of Camp Topridge Member Program, 2010, p. 12.
55. Ibid.
56. Spottswood P. Dudley Oral History, p. 5.
57. Memories of Camp Topridge Member Program, 2010, p. 12.
58. Spottswood P. Dudley Oral History, p. 3.
59. Memories of Camp Topridge Member Program, 2010, pp. 12-13.
60. Ibid.
61. Spottswood P. Dudley Oral History, p. 7.
62. Stanley Rumbough Oral History, p. 9.
63. Dina Merrill Hartley Oral History #2, p. 6.
64. Ibid.
65. Kathy and Harlan Crow, Camp Topridge Collection.
66. Nina Rumbough Oral History, p. 9.
67. Lawrence Lester Oral History, p. 3.
68. Ibid, p. 4.
69. Ibid, p. 5.
70. Kathy and Harlan Crow, Camp Topridge Collection.
71. Lawrence Lester Oral History, p. 18.
72. Camp Topridge folders, Post Family Collection.
73. Lawrence Lester Oral History, p. 7.
74. Stanley Rumbough Oral History, pp. 9, 15.
75. Camp Topridge folders, Post Family Collection.
76. Nina Rumbough Oral History, p. 4.
77. Lawrence Lester Oral History, p. 7
78. Memories of Camp Topridge Member Program, 2010, pp. 10-11.
79. Lawrence Lester Oral History, p. 11.
80. Memories of Camp Topridge Member Program, 2010, pp. 10-11.
81. Dina Merrill Hartley Oral History #2, pp. 4-5.
82. Memories of Camp Topridge Member Program, 2010, pp. 10-11.
83. Camp Topridge folders, Post Family Collection.
84. Ellen Charles, Memories of Camp Topridge Member Program, 2010, p. 14.

### Autumn

1. Earl Loy Oral History, p. 3.
2. Donald E. Handelman Oral History, p. 11; Gus Modig Oral History #2, p. 12.
3. Earl Loy Oral History, p. 3.
4. Donald E. Handelman Oral History, p. 11.
5. Hillwood Staff Quarters folder, Post Family Collection.
6. Donald E. Handelman Oral History, p. 5.
7. Hillwood Appliance inventory, Post Family Collection.
8. Earl Loy Oral History, p. 7.
9. Ibid.
10. Earl Loy Oral History, pp. 12-13.
11. Gus Modig Oral History #2, p. 2
12. Ibid, pp. 5-6.
13. Earl Loy Oral History, p. 19.
14. Earl Loy interview with the author, October 4, 2011.
15. Gabriele Weinert Oral History, p. 14.
16. Gus Modig Oral History #2, pp. 5, 6.
17. Earl Loy Oral History, p. 35.
18. Ibid, p. 39.
19. Ibid, p. 20.
20. Betty Cannella Oral History, p. 30.
21. Gus Modig Oral History #2, p. 26.
22. Hillwood Food Costs and Hillwood Staff Quarters folders, Post Family Collection.
23. Ellen Charles Oral History, p. 19.
24. Walter Beach Oral History, p. 26.
25. Ellen Charles Oral History, p. 19.
26. Betty Cannella Oral History, p. 12.
27. Donald E. Handelman Oral History, p. 8.
28. Ibid, p. 26.
29. Betty Cannella Oral History, p. 24.
30. Earl Loy Oral History, p. 40.
31. Ibid, p. 12.
32. Ibid, p. 7.
33. Mrs. Merriweather Post, "Notes on Organization," January 1965, Post Family Collection.
34. Ibid.
35. Stephen Vanilio Oral History, p. 3.
36. Ibid, p. 10.
37. Stephen Vanilio Oral History, pp. 12-13, 23; John Greenawalt Oral History, p. 26.
38. Gus Modig Oral History #2, p. 16.
39. Marjorie Merriweather Post, *Notes on Hillwood*, p. 1.
40. Marvin Ross, *The Art of Karl Fabergé and His Contemporaries*, p. viii.
41. Paul Schaffer Oral History, p. 67.
42. Amy Ballard Oral History, p. 12.
43. Scampi folder, Post Family Collection. Hillwood Object Record 31.104.
44. Gus Modig Oral History #2, p. 16.
45. Ibid, p. 17.
46. Betty Cannella Oral History, p. 23.
47. Ibid, p. 24.
48. Charles Mortimer, Interview by Nettie Major, August 8, 1965. Post Family Collection.
49. Ibid.
50. Ibid.
51. Stewart Bankert Oral History, pp. 16-17.
52. Transcript of interview with David Zeitlin, *Life* magazine, 1964, Post Family Collection.
53. Ibid.
54. Gabriele Weinert Oral History, p. 15.

55. Marilyn Holt, *Mamie Doud Eisenhower*, p. 81. Karal Ann Marling, *As Seen on TV*, pp. 38, 40, 41.
56. Hillwood Appliances, Post Family Collection. Liana Paredes, *Sèvres Porcelain at Hillwood*, p. 12. Marvin Ross, *The Art of Karl Fabergé and His Contemporaries*, pp. vii, viii.
57. Earl Loy Oral History, p. 30.
58. Stephanie Brown, "In the Event of a National Emergency: Marjorie Merriweather Post's Fallout Shelters," pp. 1, 3, 7.
59. Earl Loy Oral History, pp. 29, 30, 35.
60. Manuel Diaz interview with the author, April 2012.
61. James Patterson, *Grand Expectations*, p. 678.
62. Howard Zinn, *The Twentieth Century*, p. 206; James Patterson, *Grand Expectations*, pp. 678–702.
63. Letter to Ake Jonsson, Post Family Collection.
64. Stewart Bankert Oral History, p. 2.
65. Ibid.
66. Ibid, p. 34.
67. Ibid, p. 17.
68. Ibid, p. 18.
69. Rose Dickens Oral History, p. 6.
70. Ibid.
71. Ibid, p. 7.
72. Ibid, pp. 4–5.
73. Ibid, p. 5.
74. Earl Loy folder, Post Family Collection.
75. Handelman folder, Post Family Collection.
76. Gus Modig and Nettie Major folder, Post Family Collection.
77. Handelman folder, Post Family Collection.
78. Hillwood Flagstaff Dedication folder, Hillwood Flagpole presentation album Box 53, Post Family Collection. Contributors included staff at husband Herbert May's Rosewall estate in Pittsburgh.
79. Ibid.
80. Ibid.
81. Ibid.
82. Ibid.

## Winter

1. Lady Bird Johnson, *White House Diary*, p. 647.
2. "Society: Mumsy the Magnificent," *Time*, February 3, 1967.
3. Nina Rumbough Oral History, p. 5.
4. Spottswood Dudley Oral History, p. 14.
5. Betty Beale, "Capitalites Frolic in Palm Beach," March 12, 1956.
6. Nettie Major, "Mar-A-Lago, Palm Beach Florida," 1969.
7. Ibid.
8. "The Breakers History," pamphlet, 2012.
9. Susan Braden, *The Architecture of Leisure*, pp. 324, 326–37.
10. Margaret Carroll, "A Queen in her Palace in Palm Beach," *Chicago Today*, April 13, 1971.
11. Dina Merrill Hartley Oral History #1, p. 31.
12. Historic American Buildings Survey FLA-195, 1967.
13. Ibid.
14. James Griffin Jr. Oral History, p. 6.
15. Ibid, p. 2.
16. Griffin folder, Post Family Collection.
17. James Griffin Jr. Oral History, pp. 32–33.
18. "The Breakers History," pamphlet, 2012. Mar-A-Lago folders, Post Family Collection.
19. Nettie Major, "Mar-A-Lago, Palm Beach Florida," 1969.
20. Mrs. Merriweather Post, "Notes on Organization," January 1965, Post Family Collection.
21. James Griffin Jr. Oral History, p. 20; Gabriele Weinert Oral History, p. 12.
22. James Griffin Jr. Oral History, p. 34.
23. Betty Cannella Oral History, p. 9.
24. Gabriele Weinert Oral History, p. 4.
25. Ibid, pp. 1, 2, 9.
26. Suzy, "Mrs. Post Stole the Show," *Palm Beach Daily News*, January 22, 1971.
27. Stanley Rumbough Oral History, p. 8.
28. Ibid, p. 11; Nina Rumbough Oral History, p. 1.
29. Mar-A-Lago folders, Post Family Collection.
30. Nina Rumbough Oral History, p. 5.
31. Spottswood Dudley Oral History, p. 8; Nettie Major, "Mar-A-Lago, Palm Beach Florida," 1969.
32. Michael and Maria Abate Oral History, p. 34.
33. Spottswood Dudley Oral History, p. 2.
34. Ibid.
35. Ibid, p. 3.
36. Nettie Major, "Mar-A-Lago, Palm Beach Florida," 1969.
37. Ibid.
38. James Griffin Jr. Oral History, p. 31.
39. Nettie Major, "Mar-A-Lago, Palm Beach Florida," 1969.
40. Becky Rogers, Mrs. Post Memories Program, March 1, 2011. Dina Merrill Hartley Oral History #2, 2010, pp. 11–12.
41. James Griffin Jr. Oral History, p. 24.
42. Kennedy folders and Mar-A-Lago General folder, Post Family Collection.
43. Nina Rumbough Oral History, pp. 4–6.
44. Suzy, "Mrs. Post Looked Like a Hundred Million," *Palm Beach Post*, March 16, 1970.
45. James Griffin Jr. Oral History, p. 25.
46. Ibid.
47. Ibid, p. 26.
48. Nettie Major, "Mar-A-Lago, Palm Beach Florida," 1969.
49. James Griffin Jr. Oral History, pp. 28–29.
50. Nettie Major, "Mar-A-Lago, Palm Beach Florida," 1969.
51. Mar-A-Lago folders, Post Family Collection.
52. Lady Bird Johnson folder, Post Family Collection.
53. Historic American Buildings Survey FLA-195, 1967.
54. Animal Rescue League folder, Post Family Collection.
55. James Griffin Jr. Oral History, p. 14.
56. Animal Rescue League, Good Samaritan Ball, Mar-A-Lago General folder, Post Family Collection.

57. Ibid.
58. Ibid.
59. Mar-A-Lago folders, Post Family Collection.
60. Ibid.
61. John Convery Oral History, p. 18.
62. Ibid, p. 2.
63. Sigma Alpha Epsilon folder, Post Family Collection.
64. Michael Tucci Oral History, p. 4.
65. John Convery Oral History, p. 10.
66. Ibid.
67. Michael Tucci Oral History, p. 6.
68. Ibid.
69. John Convery Oral History, p. 11.
70. Michael Tucci Oral History, p. 27.
71. Ibid, p. 5.
72. James Griffin Jr. Oral History, p. 38.
73. Red Cross Ball 1964, 1966, 1967, and 1969 folders, Post Family Collection; "The Golden Anniversary of the International Red Cross Ball," *Black Tie*, n.d., 2007.
74. Gabriele Weinert Oral History, p. 3.
75. Red Cross Ball 1964, 1966, 1967, and 1969 folders, Post Family Collection.
76. Red Cross Ball 1967 folder, Post Family Collection.
77. Gabriele Weinert Oral History, p. 8; Lady Bird Johnson folder, Post Family Collection.
78. Lady Bird Johnson folder, Post Family Collection.
79. Betty Beale, "Yule Gift from Mrs. Post," *Washington Evening Star*, January 3, 1968.
80. James Griffin Jr. Oral History, pp. 50–51.
81. Christmas List books, Hillwood Archives.
82. James Griffin Jr. Oral History, p. 33; Griffin folder, Post Family Collection.
83. Spottswood Dudley Oral History, p. 12.

# Bibliography

**Hillwood Art Research Library, Archives, and Visual Resources**

Michael and Maria Abate Oral History, an interview conducted by Stephanie Brown, November 16, 2005

Amy Ballard Oral History, an interview conducted by Estella M. Chung, December 7, 2001.

Stewart Bankert Oral History, an interview conducted by Kathi Ann Brown, September 9, 1997.

Walter Beach Oral History, an interview conducted by Stephanie Brown, November 6, 2003.

Betty Beale Oral History, an interview conducted by Stephanie Brown, January 23, 2004.

Beale, Betty. *Power at Play*. Washington, D.C.: Regnery Gateway, 1993.

Braden, Susan. *The Architecture of Leisure: The Florida Resort Hotels of Henry Flagler and Henry Plant*. Tallahassee: University Press of Florida, 2002.

Peggy Brown Oral History, an interview conducted by Kathi Ann Brown, September 10, 1997.

Brown, Stephanie. "Descendants of Charles William Post," Hillwood Archives, 2006.

Brown, Stephanie. "In the Event of a National Emergency: Marjorie Merriweather Post's Fallout Shelters," Hillwood Archives, 2006.

Betty Cannella Oral History, an interview conducted by Nancy Harris, November 2, 1998.

Rodion Cantacuzene Oral History, an interview conducted by Kathi Ann Brown, September 9, 1997.

Hill Carter Oral History, an interview conducted by Nancy Harris, April 19, 1999.

Ellen Charles interview with Estella M. Chung, February 23, 2012.

Ellen Charles Oral History, an interview conducted by Stephanie Brown, November 13, 2003.

Christmas List books, Hillwood Archives.

Jennifer Conover Oral History, an interview conducted by Kathi Ann Brown, October 23, 1997.

John Convery Oral History, an interview conducted by Estella M. Chung, July 8, 2009.

Rose Dickens Oral History, an interview conducted by Stephanie Brown, May 13, 2004.

Davies, Emlen Knight. "My Journey," in Emlen Knight Davies and Mia Grosjean, *A Photographic Journey of the Ambassador's Daughter: Moscow, 1937–38*. Washington, D.C.: Hillwood Museum and Gardens, 2010. An exhibition catalog.

Bibliography

Spottswood P. Dudley Oral History, an interview conducted by Estella M. Chung, December 6, 2011.

General Foods. *Joys of Jell-O*. 1963.

John Greenawalt Oral History, an interview conducted by Estella M. Chung, May 21, 2010.

James Griffin Jr. Oral History, an interview conducted by Nancy Harris, May 27, 1998.

Donald E. Handelman Oral History, an interview conducted by Kathi Ann Brown, June 3, 1998.

Dina Merrill Hartley Oral History #1, an interview conducted by Stephanie Brown, February 5, 2004.

Dina Merrill Hartley Oral History #2, an interview conducted by Estella M. Chung, September 29, 2010.

Heymann, C. David. *The Georgetown Ladies Social Club*. New York: Atria Books, 2003.

Holt, Marilyn. *Mamie Doud Eisenhower*. Lawrence: University Press of Kansas, 2007.

Johnson, Lady Bird. *A White House Diary*. New York: Holt, Rinehart, and Winston, 1970.

Kaiser, Harvey. *Great Camps of the Adirondacks*. Boston: Godine, 1982.

Lawrence Lester Oral History, an interview conducted by Estella M. Chung, June 24, 2010.

Earl Loy Oral History, an interview conducted by Stephanie Brown, May 14, 2004.

Marling, Karal Ann. *As Seen on TV*. Cambridge, MA: Harvard University Press, 1994.

Memories of Camp Topridge Member Program, 2010.

Mesta, Perle Skirvin. *Perle: My Story*. New York: McGraw-Hill, 1960.

Gus Modig Oral History #1, an interview conducted by Anne Odom and Liana Paredes, January 29, 1999.

Gus Modig Oral History #2, an interview conducted by Anne Odom and Liana Paredes, February 11, 1999.

Gus Modig Oral History #3, an interview conducted by Anne Odom and Liana Paredes, February 19, 1999.

Frank Del Monte Oral History, an interview conducted by Stephanie Brown, February 17, 2004.

Frank Del Monte Jr., "Mrs. Post's Limo," Hillwood Archives.

Mulford, Nancy Perot. "Adirondack: Camp Topridge Evolves," Hillwood director clippings files.

Paredes, Liana. *Sèvres Porcelain at Hillwood*. Washington, D.C.: Hillwood Museum and Gardens, 1998.

Patterson, James. *Grand Expectations*. New York: Oxford University Press, 1996.

Photograph Collection, Hillwood Archives.

Post, Marjorie Merriweather. *Notes on Hillwood*. Washington, D.C.: Corporate Press, 1970.

Newspaper Clippings File, Hillwood Archives.

Becky Rogers, Mrs. Post Memories Program, March 1, 2011.

Ross, Marvin. *The Art of Karl Fabergé and His Contemporaries*. Norman: University of Oklahoma Press, 1965.

Rubin, Nancy. *American Empress*. Lincoln, NE: iUniverse Star, 2004.

Nina Rumbough Oral History, an interview conducted by Estella M. Chung, September 30, 2010.

Stanley Rumbough Oral History, an interview conducted by Estella M. Chung, September 16, 2011.

Paul Schaffer Oral History, an interview conducted by Stephanie Brown, February 6, 2004.

Lisa Smith Oral History, an interview conducted by Estella M. Chung, August 25, 2009.

Marshall Thompson Oral History, an interview conducted by Stephanie Brown, October 22, 2003.

Michael Tucci Oral History, an interview conducted by Estella M. Chung, November 4, 2011.

Stephen Vanilio Oral History, an interview conducted by Estella M. Chung, May 17, 2010.

Gabriele Weinert Oral History, an interview conducted by Estella M. Chung, October 6, 2009.

Vera Whalen Oral History, an interview conducted by Stephanie Brown, March 25, 2006.

Zinn, Howard. *The Twentieth Century*. New York: HarperCollins, 2003.

**Other sources**

"A World Unique and Magnificent," *Life*, November 5, 1965.

Barron, James. "Evangeline Bruce, 77, Hostess Known for Washington Soirees," *New York Times*, December 14, 1995.

Beale, Betty. "Capitalites Frolic in Palm Beach," *Washington Evening Star*, March 12, 1956.

Beale, Betty. "Yule Gift from Mrs. Post," *Washington Evening Star*, January 3, 1968.

"The Breakers History," pamphlet, 2012

"Camp Topridge Revisited," *Architectural Digest*, June 1999.

# Bibliography

Carroll, Margaret. "A Queen in her Palace in Palm Beach," *Chicago Today*, April 13, 1971.

Kathy and Harlan Crow, Camp Topridge Collection.

Fenzi, Jewell. "Elizabeth Moffat White: An Interview," July 26, 1988, Association for Diplomatic Studies and Training Foreign Affairs Oral History Program Foreign Service Spouse Series, Library of Congress.

Fenzi, Jewell, and Allidi Black. *Democratic Women: An Oral History of the Woman's National Democratic Club*. Washington, D.C.: WNDC Educational Foundation, 2000.

General Foods Kitchens. *Baker's Chocolate and Coconut Favorites*, 1965.

"The Golden Anniversary of the International Red Cross Ball," *Black Tie*, n.d., 2007.

Historic American Buildings Survey FLA-195, 1967.

Jones, Margaret. "Money: Women Hold 80 P.C. of Big Fortunes," *Boston Globe*, January 30, 1966.

Jacqueline Kennedy Oral History, University of Kentucky, May 13, 1981.

MacPherson, Myra. "Mrs. Post Serves Tea—for 300," *New York Times*, May 26, 1966.

Major, Nettie. "Mar-A-Lago, Palm Beach Florida," 1969.

McCardle, Dorothy. "Along With a Gift Mrs. Post Gives a Laundry Lesson," *Washington Post*, November 22, 1966.

McCardle, Dorothy. "Orchestra Plays Upbeat Evening for Mrs. Post," *Washington Post*, March 16, 1967.

"Mrs. Post is Host to Veterans," *Washington Evening Star*, May 5, 1970.

"Perennial Party Blooms into Weekend," *Washington Post*, May 1, 1967.

Post Family Collection, Bentley Historical Library, University of Michigan.

Mrs. Merriweather Post, "Notes on Organization," January 1965.

Radcliffe, Donnie. "The Witty Mrs. Post: Belle of Umpteen Symphony Balls," *Washington Star*, November 23, 1969.

Schaden, Herman. "Symphony Summer Home to Honor Backer," *Washington Post*, September 28, 1966.

"Society: Mumsy the Magnificent," *Time*, February 3, 1967.

"Sorority Sisters' Luxury Weekend," *Life*, May 16, 1960.

Suzy. "If Mrs. Post Says Formal it IS Formal," *Miami Herald*, November 21, 1967.

Suzy. "Mrs. Post Looked Like a Hundred Million," *Palm Beach Post*, March 16, 1970.

Suzy. "Mrs. Post Stole the Show," *Palm Beach Daily News*, January 22, 1971.

Woman's National Democratic Club Archive, Washington, D.C.

Women of General Foods Kitchens. *The General Foods Kitchens Cookbook*. New York: Random House, 1959.

**Consultations—
Hillwood Board and Staff**

Brian Barr, Ellen Charles, Manuel Diaz, Angie Dodson, Bill Johnson, Howard Kurtz, Liana Paredes, Kirsten Regina, Manuel Rouco, Scott Ruby

## Photo credits

Unless otherwise noted, images are © Hillwood Estate, Museums & Gardens.

p. 2: Alfred Eisenstaedt/Time & Life Pictures/Getty Images
p. 17 top right (*Merriweather* jet interior): Bentley Historical Library, University of Michigan
p. 25: Alfred Eisenstaedt/Time & Life Pictures/Getty Images
p. 28: Alfred Eisenstaedt/Time & Life Pictures/Getty Images
p. 29: Alfred Eisenstaedt/Time & Life Pictures/Getty Images
p. 31: Alfred Eisenstaedt/Time & Life Pictures/Getty Images
p. 35 right: Horst/Brand © Condé Nast 1957
p. 43: Bentley Historical Library, University of Michigan
p. 44: Bentley Historical Library, University of Michigan
p. 58: Bentley Historical Library, University of Michigan
p. 77: Alfred Eisenstaedt/Time & Life Pictures/Getty Images
p. 79: Alfred Eisenstaedt/Time & Life Pictures/Getty Images
p. 85: Alfred Eisenstaedt/Time & Life Pictures/Getty Images
p. 112 bottom: Alfred Eisenstaedt/Time & Life Pictures/Getty Images
pp. 116/117: Alfred Eisenstaedt/Time & Life Pictures/Getty Images
p. 120 right: Alfred Eisenstaedt/Time & Life Pictures/Getty Images

# Index

Pages numbers in *italics* indicate illustrations.
'MMP' refers to Marjorie Merriweather Post

## A
Abate, Tony (Oldrich Royce), 108, 111
airplanes. *See Merriweather* jet
Alphand, Hervé (French ambassador), *21*
amethyst necklace and earrings (Cartier), 106, *106*
*The Art of Karl Fabergé* (Ross), 84
Ault, Clyde (Hillwood general manager), 49, 57, 92

## B
Bankert, Stewart (hairdresser), 93–94
Barzin, Leon (son-in-law), 44
Beach, Walter (guest at Hillwood and Topridge), 36, 53, 55
Beale, Betty (social columnist), 30, 36, 39, 42, 52, 55, 100
Benham, Frank (dancer), 61
boats, 53, 54–55, 62, *63*, 67, *67*, 96
The Boulders, Greenwich, Connecticut, 13, *13*
bracelet (David Webb), *106*
The Breakers hotel, Palm Beach, Florida, 100, 104
Brown, John Alden (guest), 70
Brown, Peggy (neighbor at Hillwood), 30, 43
Bruce, Evangeline (political hostess), 42

## C
C. W. Post College, Long Island University, New York, 45, 48, *119*, 120
Camp Topridge, Adirondacks, New York State, 52, 53, *70–71*
    bathmat, *57*
    collections, 57, *58*
    house parties
        the "carry", 67, *67*, *68*, *69*, 69–70
        dancing, *18*, 53, 61, *61*
        family holidays, 52, 54, 61, 63, 64–65, 66, 67, 69–70
        film shows, 65–67, *66*
        invited guests, 52–53, 54–55, *55*, 59, *59*, 61, 62–63, 65–67, 70
        meals, 59, *59*, 61–62, 65, 67, 69, 69–70, *128*
        outdoor activities, *62*, 62–64, *63*, 65, 67, *67*, *68*, *69*, 69–70
    MMP as hostess, 52–53, 62, 70
    rooms and cabins
        Big Room, 55, 57, *58*, 62
        boathouse and cottage, 55, *55*, *56*
        dacha, *60*, 61
        dining room, *59*
        guest accommodation, 53, *53*, 55
        main lodge, *52*, *57*, 57
        MMP's cabin, *57*, 65
        staff accommodation, 53, 53–54, *54*
    staff, 52, 53–54, 55, 62–63, 64, 65, 67, *68*
    wallpaper, *59*
Cannella, Betty (financial secretary), 80, 81, 87, 90
Cantacuzene, Rodion (grandson-in-law), 24, 43
Carroll, Margaret *(Chicago Today)*, 103
cars, 17, 18, *20*, 54
Catherine the Great Easter egg (Fabergé), *13*, 91
Charles, Ellen (granddaughter)
    on Camp Topridge, 52, 54, 61, 63, 64, 67, 69, 70
    on Hillwood meals, 32
    on MMP, 15, 32, 81
Chips, Doris (bookbinder), 82
clock (Fabergé), 91
Close, Adelaide (daughter), 15
Close, Edward (first husband), 15
Close, Eleanor (daughter), 15
Conover, Jennifer (step-granddaughter), 20
Constitution Hall, Washington, D. C., 44, *44*
Convery, John (C. W. Post College student), 120, 123
Cronk, Charles (security officer), 96

## D
Davies, Joseph (third husband), 15, 76, *126*
Del Monte, Frank (driver), 18
Dickens, Rose (manicurist), 94–95
Dudley, Henry (guest and estate planner), 111
Dudley, Spottswood P. (guest), 17, 62–63, 64, 100, 111, 112, 126

## E
Eisenhower, Dwight D. and Mamie, 42, 91
Eisenstaedt, Alfred (*Life* magazine photographer), 48

## F
Fabergé, Karl, *11*, *13*, 84, 91
Field, Arthur (Hillwood footman), 27, *28*
Fulton, James G. (Pennsylvania congressman), 96

## G
General Foods, *12*, 12–13, 61, 81, 87, 90, 92
Good Seasons mixes (General Foods), 90
Grape Nuts cereal (General Foods), 12, 61, *79*, 80
Griffin, James (Mar-A-Lago superintendent), 103
Griffin, James, Jr. ("Jimmy", Mar-A-Lago superintendent), 15, 17, 103, 104, 114, 115, 123, 124, 126

## H
Handelman, Donald (financial manager), 19–20, 74, 75, 81
Handelman, Meyer (financial manager), 81, 95–96
Hartley, Dina Merrill. *See* Merrill, Dina
Heurtematte, Julio (Topridge guest), 54, 61
Hillwood, Washington, D.C., 24, *35*, *40–41*, 74
    chair covers, 15
    charitable events, 24, 44
    closing, 15, *16*, 17
    collections, 20
        dinner services, *26*, 26–27, 32
        French 18th and 19th century art, 7, 13, *14*, 26–27, 82, 84
        glass, 30, 82
        porcelain, *12*, *14*, 26, 27, 30, 82, 84
        Russian art, 7, 13, *13*, 26, 27, 82, 84, 95, *95*
        silver, 12, 27
        table linen, 26, 30, 75, 95, *96*
    cooking, *31*, 32, 80
    fallout shelters, 92, *92*, 93
    film shows, 36
    financial matters, 80–81

flagpole presentation ceremony, 96, *97*
flower arrangements, *26*, 30, 76, 80
formal dinners, 24, 26–27, 30, *30*, 32, 36
    menus, 24, 26, *26*, 36
        table settings, *14*, *26*, 26–27, 30, 36
        garden parties, 24, *24*, *26*, 36, 39, 43, *43*, 81
gardens, *48*, *49*, 74, *75*, 76, *77*, *81*, 81–82, *82*
improvements and renovations, 74–75, 92, 93–94
linen books, 26, *27*
meals, 76, *79*, 80, 84, 87
MMP as hostess, 24, 26–27, 30, 32, 36, 39,̈ 42, 48, 95
MMP on care of linen, 43, 95, *96*
MMP's daily routine, 76, 80, 81–82, 84, 87, 90–91
motor court, *24*, *40–41*
and 1968 riots, 92–93
pet cemetery, 84, *84*
putting green, 81, *81*
rooms
    breakfast room, 76, 80, *80*, 81, 84, 87
    butler's pantry, 26, 27, 32, 75, *79*
    entrance hall, 32, *33*, 76
    French drawing room, 32, *34*, *134*
    icon room, *39*
    kitchen, *31*, *75*, 75–76
    library, *82–83*, *86*, 87, *87*
    MMP's bathroom, *91*, 91–92
    MMP's bedroom, *88–89*, 90, *90*, 91
    MMP's dressing room, 24, *26*, 76
    pavilion, 30, 36, *37*, *38*, 48
    staff accommodation, 74, 75, *75*, 76, 80
servicemen as guests, *43*, 43–44, 93
sound system, 39, *39*
staff, 24, 27, 32, 49, 74, 75, *75*, 76, 80, 82, 95–96, *97*
staircase, *33*, *78*
trunks, *18*
Hillwood Museum, Washington, D.C., 20, 114
"Hillwood service" (Gotham), *12*
Hutton, E. F. (second husband), 15
Hutton, Nedenia (daughter, later Dina Merrill), *15*

## J
Jell-O (General Foods), *12*, 61, 65, 81
Johnson, Lady Bird, 42, 49, *49*, 52, 100, 116, *123*, 124, *125*

## K
Kawatch, Frank (film projectionist), 66
Kennedy, Jackie, *16*, 39, 42, 82
Kennedy, John F., *16*, 45, 92
Kennedy, Rose, 45, 114,̈ *120*
Korth, Fred (Navy Secretary), *122*

## L
Lester, Lawrence (Topridge staff member), 53–54, 65, 66, 67
*Life* magazine, 45, 48
Louis Vuitton trunk, *18*
Loy, Earl (Hillwood gardener), 43, 76, *77*, 80, 81, 82, 92, 95

## M
MacMaster, Federico (dancer), 61, 115
Major, Nettie Leitch (hired writer), 100
Mann, James (Hillwood general manager), 49, 80
Mar-A-Lago, Palm Beach, Florida, 100, *100*, 103
    building, 104, 112, 116
    charitable events, 103, *114*, 116, 119, *122*, 123
    Christmas, 124, 126, *127*
    cloisters, *102*, *110*
    fallout shelters, 116
    floors, protecting, *115*, 115–16
    garden, *103*, 104, *104*
    house parties, 104, 106
        family holidays, 103, 106, 108
        invited guests, 100, 103, 104, 108, 111–12, 114, *120*, 123, 124
        students, 119, 120, 123
    MMP as hostess, 52, 100, 103, 108, 114, 119, *120*, *120*, 123
    parties, 103, *114*, 114–16, *116–17*
    *pierre dure* table, 112, *112*, *113*, 114
    rooms
        Dina Merrill's suite, 108, *108*, *109*, 124
        dining room, 112, *112*
        entrance hall, *100*
        guest suites, 100, 103, *107*, 108, *109*, 111
        living room, 115, *118*, *140*
        MMP's bedroom, *104–5*
        patio, 104, 108, 115–16, *121*
        pavilion, 116, *116–17*
        staff accommodation, 103–4
    sheets, *111*
    spiral columns, *101*, 104
    staff, 103, 104, 106, 126
    statues, *101*, *103*
    student visitors, 119, 120, 123
    tower, 108, *110*, 111
Mark, Statia (dancer), 61
May, Herbert (fourth husband), 15
McNutt, Louise (Hillwood guest), *38*
Merrill, Dina (Nedenia Hutton), 7, 15, *15*, 17, 87
    on Camp Topridge, 52, 57, 61, 64, 69
    at Hillwood, *30*
    on Mar-A-Lago, 103, 108, *108*
Merriweather, Ella (mother), 12
*Merriweather* boat, 53, 54–55
*Merriweather* jet, *17*, 17–18, 52, 53, 54, 70, 104, 123
Merriweather Post Pavilion of Music, Columbia, Maryland, 44–45
Mesta, Perle (political hostess), 39
Modig, Gus ("Mr. Gus", Hillwood butler), 24, *25*, 26, 27, *29*, 30, 32, 36, 44, 74, 76, 80, 95
Moffat, Frank (Topridge steward), 54
Mortimer, Charles (General Foods), 90
"Music for Young America" series, 44

## N
National Symphony Orchestra, Washington, D. C., 44–45
Nehru, Fori (wife of B. K. Nehru), 12

# Index

Nixon, Pat, 42
*Notes on Hillwood* (MMP), 84

## P
Peruvian ambassador, *24*
Post, Charles William ("C. W.", father), 12, 13
Post, Marjorie Merriweather, *15, 19, 35, 38, 122*
    animals, love of, 65, 84, 116
    and C. W. Post College, 45, 48, *119,* 120
    character, 18–19, 20, 30, 39, 76, 90, 94–96
    charities and fundraising, 13, 24, 44, 49, 81, 116
    as a Christian Scientist, 36
    Christmas and Christmas gifts, 124, 126, *126*
    commitment to work, 19, 49, 81, 87–88, 90, 119
    dances and dancing, *18,* 61, *61, 114,* 115
    director of General Foods, 12, 61, 81, 87
    eightieth birthday celebrations, 44, *44*
    hair and hairdressing, 90, 93–94, *94*
    hats, 18, *20*
    jewelry, *99,* 106, *106,* 123
    Legion of Honor, *21*
    manicures, 94, *95*
    marriages and children, 15, *15*
    as "Mommyda" (grandmother), 64, 65, 66, 108
    pink, love of, 91
    as a planner, 7, 13, 20, 24
    on running households, 13, 15, 17–20
    sleep, need for, 91
    superstitions, 114
Post Toasties cereal (General Foods), 12, 61, *93*
Postum coffee substitute (General Foods), 12, 36, 61
Pratt, Major General H. Conger and Sadie, *57*

## R
Radcliffe, Donnie *(Washington Post),* 44
Red Cross Ball, Mar-A-Lago, *122,* 123–24, *124*
Robertson, Cliff (son-in-law), *30*
Ross, Marvin (Hillwood curator), 57, 63, 84, *84*
"round-and-square" dances, 61, *61, 116–17*
Rumbough, Nina (granddaughter), 52, 64, 65, 66, 100, 108, 114–15
Rumbough, Stanley (grandson), 52, 61, 64, 66, 106
Russell, Ed (Topridge caretaker), 54, 57, 62
Russian nuptial crown, *95*
*Russian Porcelains* (Ross), 84

## S
Saint-Gobain heated towel rack, 91
Scampi (miniature schnauzer), *77,* 84, *85,* 106, 124
Sèvres porcelain, *14*
Smith, Lisa (C. W. Post College student), 45, 48
Spectacle Lake, Adirondacks, New York State, *52,* 62
square-dances, *18,* 53, 61, 114, 120
Sugar Crisp cereal (General Foods), 12, *93*
*Suzy (Miami Herald),* 27, 30, 32

## T
Tucci, Michael (C. W. Post college student), 120, 123

## U
Urban, Joseph (architect of Mar-A-Lago), 112

## V
Voigt, Margaret (social secretary), 24, 43, 63, 64, 80, 87, 119

## W
Washington social scene, 24, 36, 39, 42–43, 74
Weinert, Gabriele (personal maid), 17–18, 91, 104, 106, 123
Winston, Harry, *99*
Woman's National Democratic Club, 43
Wyeth, Marion (architect of Mar-A-Lago), 112, 116

## Z
Zackrisson, Eva (personal maid), 76, 80, 90
Zeitlin, David (*Life* magazine), 13, 48